rachel
a stolen life

rachel
a stolen life

WANDA MORAN

JB

JOHN BLAKE

Published by John Blake Publishing Ltd,
3 Bramber Court, 2 Bramber Road,
London W14 9PB, England

www.blake.co.uk

First published in hardback in 2007

ISBN: 978-1-84454-340-3

British Library Cataloguing-in-Publication Data:

A catalogue record for this book is available from the British Library.

Design by www.envydesign.co.uk

Printed in Great Britain by Creative Print & Design, Ebbw Vale, Wales

1 3 5 7 9 10 8 6 4 2

Papers used by John Blake Publishing are natural, recyclable products made from
wood grown in sustainable forests. The manufacturing processes conform to the
environmental regulations of the country of origin.

All pictures from the author's collection

This book is dedicated to Vanda, my daughter, my friend, without whom Rachel's story would never have been told.

Foreword

The abduction and murder of Rachel Moran during the early hours of New Year's Day 2003 was one of the most shocking crimes in Hull in recent years.

She was a 21-year-old woman from a loving, Catholic family snatched from the street as she walked home from a party and stabbed to death, seemingly without reason. Her killer, Michael Little, was a loner who happened to live nearby. Rachel hadn't met him before. She was simply in the wrong place at the wrong time.

I got to know the family through covering the case in my role at the time as crime reporter for the *Hull and East Riding Mail* and spent many hours in their company, talking about Rachel and what she meant to them. Throughout their ordeal, they conducted themselves with the utmost dignity.

During the weeks she was missing, they did everything they could to assist the police investigation and help media appeals for information. They welcomed me into their home from the start. I was a stranger who came into their lives in the most terrible of circumstances but they were never anything other than completely co-operative. I spoke to the family most days during the four weeks between Rachel being reported missing and the police finding her body at Little's flat. We got to know each other well.

Publicly, they clung to the hope Rachel would return home safe and well. As the days and weeks passed though, it became clear there would be no happy ending. They knew it and so did I.

Yet they never fell apart. They stayed strong for each other.

I was, and still am, amazed by the individual and collective strength they showed throughout. They are a remarkable family. The day Rachel's body was found was one of the worst of my professional life. I was outside Little's flat trying to interview neighbours about the gruesome discovery but could only think about Rachel's family and what they must be going through. They were decent, hard working people who had been plunged into the most devastating of tragedies.

When Little was eventually convicted of Rachel's murder, after the most dramatic court case I have witnessed, senior police officers and court staff broke down in tears. I struggled to contain my own emotions and I know colleagues also covering the trial were the same. I have covered numerous murders for the newspaper, but none have affected me as much as Rachel's.

Her senseless killing impacted on so many lives. At the centre of it all was her mother. Wanda spoke little of her own feelings throughout, but she talked constantly about Rachel. She reminisced about the good times and bad, and of the hopes she had for her future. But she gave hardly anything away about her own trauma. She didn't talk about the devastating impact Rachel's brutal death had on her personally. I had no idea at the time she was writing it all down in her diaries.

Wanda began writing as a form of therapy, to try and come to terms with the loss of her youngest daughter. She didn't intend for them to be published. Her diaries allowed her to express her private emotions when her life was falling apart around her. It was only on the advice of daughter Vanda she realised hers was a story that deserved to be shared with a wider audience.

At times, her diaries make for harrowing reading. In a startlingly honest account, Wanda reveals the full horror of the search for Rachel. She details the moment she was told her daughter's body was found and the anguish of burying her. As one of the last people to have seen her alive, Wanda had to give evidence at crown court during Little's trial for murder. She reveals the full trauma of the experience and the pain of having to listen to Little's vicious lies as he tried to escape justice. She also tells of the suffering that will never ease.

But even out of the most devastating of tragedies shines some light. There is a determination Rachel's brutal death will not tear the rest of her family apart. And there is hope Wanda's own experiences will help others struggling to cope with loss. It is a truly moving account.

Rick Lyon
Assistant News Editor
Hull and East Riding Mail
2007

Contents

Introduction

This is a story that should not have been written and, indeed, should not have *needed* to be written. It begins in 1981, the year in which my daughter, Rachel, was born and charts the life of that girl, from her birth to her untimely death 21 years later at the hands of a brutal, callous killer.

She was my youngest child and, as is so often the case with the baby of any family, she was cosseted and overindulged throughout her all too brief spell on this earth. When I bade her farewell on the eve of the New Year 2003, when she left me to make the short journey to her own home, little did I think that it would be the last time that I would ever see her.

She never completed that short journey and so began every mother's worst nightmare and it is one from which I can never awaken.

Rachel was officially a missing person for the first month

following her disappearance and continued to be so until her body was found. During these first weeks of dreadful uncertainty, I began to put into writing my own recollections of Rachel which have ultimately become the first part of this story, although of course I didn't know at the time that this would be so.

Later, in the months leading up to the trial of her murderer, I started to keep a diary of events as they unfolded and these diaries make up a large portion of this book.

For me, it was a cathartic experience, during what can only be described as the darkest days of my life. In penning my innermost thoughts and deepest fears, I was able to save my sanity and, in some small way, to assuage my grief. I continued with my diary until long after the first anniversary of Rachel's death had been and gone. I saw it as no more than a personal journal that might possibly be read by future generations of the family.

It probably would have remained as a purely personal thing had it not been for the intervention of my second daughter, Vanda. It was she who first read and then later set about transcribing my often illegible handwritten notes. She edited, added bits to and typed up what became a fairly sizeable document. She went on to convince me that Rachel's was a story worthy of publication, then did all in her power to make this happen. I owe her a debt of gratitude for her hard work and for the determination and unfailing faith she showed when I had none.

This, then, is a memorial to Rachel, my personal memories of her in life and how deeply her death and the manner of it has affected a once very ordinary family. Whenever an act of gratuitous violence is committed, it not only robs the innocent of life, but also destroys the lives of all those who loved that person. These are the secondary victims of such crimes.

I hope that, in telling Rachel's story, I have done her justice and succeeded in putting across the essence of the girl she was. My one desire is that my child will never be forgotten and that she will not end up as a mere statistic.

The Child of Our Later Years

Rachel Louise Moran came into the world shortly after 2.30am on 17 January 1981, our fourth and final child and the one who decided to arrive in the middle of the night! She also happened to be the only one born on Irish soil, making her appearance more than a month early at St James' Hospital in Dublin, a stone's throw from the famous Guinness brewery.

I was unprepared for a premature baby, so it was quite a shock for me to produce this tiny scrap of less than 7lbs, especially as my other three had all been heavyweights. She spent the first ten days of her life in an incubator, suffering from severe jaundice, but, once she was allowed home, she caught up in leaps and bounds. Indeed, in a very short time, she overtook most other babies of her age and continued to grow taller and taller, until she reached her mature height of 6ft.

Those early days were very difficult for me as an older mother without the support of family or friends near by and an often absent husband. At that time, Ray was working as a deep-sea fisherman and continued to do so for the first four or five months of Rachel's life. There was a lot of uncertainty for us at that time, as we were undecided whether we should remain in Ireland or return to the UK. The lease was due to expire on our house and Ray's job was precarious. I had sole responsibility for Rachel and three other children at various stages in their development – Kerry (17), Vanda (11) and John (six). Kerry was going through her own rebellion and studying for her final exams at school, and she was not best pleased that a new baby had come along to add to her angst. Maybe the worst aspect of it all, though, was that Vanda had just been diagnosed with the severest form of diabetes and we knew not what the future held for us.

Hardly surprising, then, that Rachel became a very demanding and unhappy baby. She probably sensed the tension in me, which consequently transferred itself to her. We finally made the decision to return to England when she was six months old and things became somewhat better. Her father secured employment in Hull that allowed him to be at home at some point during every day. The pressure was off me to some extent when he was around. However, because of the hours his job entailed, there would be many times when he would be gone long before Rachel awoke and returned long after she had been put to bed for the night. I was fortunate enough to not have to work myself so, when the others were at school or working, it was very much just the two of us alone together. It is fair to say that she remained an extremely miserable child until she was about two or three years old, when her sunny nature suddenly emerged. What a relief that was! At last I had a child I could enjoy, instead of one I could have happily throttled on many occasions.

She was in effect a lone child because of her siblings being so much older. I wanted her to have the opportunity to mix with other children so it was that, at the age of three, she started to attend a playgroup for a couple of mornings a week. She took to it like a duck to water and loved every minute, even though she was a gentle child and quite unused to the company of other small children and their exuberances.

After a year or so, we moved house and I was able to enrol her, though not without some difficulty, in a council-run nursery five afternoons a week. She loved this place even more because there were far more activities, lots more children and a chance to actually learn and not just play. The nursery, being in the University area, had its share of overseas children. One of the little girls, Shaymaa from Egypt, became Rachel's great friend. She too was a very reserved child and it was quite amusing to see the two of them together. They were born almost exactly a year apart, yet Rachel towered above Shaymaa and treated her almost like a little pet! Her love of younger, smaller children was to prevail throughout her life.

A few of the other friends she made at Lambert Street nursery were to go on with her to primary school, so she forged some relationships before she had to make the transition from the play world to the real world and all that 'big school' entailed. And so it was that Rachel's first five years flew by without too many hiccups, lots of laughter, plenty of tears, and now she was ready to start her education in earnest.

How lucky we were that, as a Catholic family, our closest primary school was St Vincent's on Queens Road. It was there that Rachel's school days began on 7 January 1986, just ten days before her fifth birthday. I remember that day so well: her school uniform, the coat she wore and even the hat I had knitted for her to wear. She was so excited and posed happily at our front door for a photograph to mark the great occasion. Both Ray and I took her along for her first day, happy for her, but sad for ourselves. Our baby had set off on her first big adventure in life and a new era had begun for us.

Very soon afterwards, I took a part-time job – the first time I had really worked since my marriage. The office was literally across the road from home and en route to the school, so I had no problems concerning Rachel's welfare. I was able to take her to school each morning before starting work and, since I left again at 2.15pm, there was even time for me to go home before returning to collect Rachel at 3.30pm. When her dad's shifts allowed, he would take or collect her, and we were fortunate to have older children who would take care of Rachel during the school holidays. It all worked very well.

Her days at St Vincent's were very happy, as it was a family-orientated school with small classes and very much a part of the parish. The teachers were, and remain, kind and caring and the headmaster knew every child by name from day one. It was a lovely community to belong to and Rachel thrived there. Father White, the parish priest, played a big part in the school, both as pastor and friend to the children. He, too, knew them all by name and loved every one of them. I like to think some of them were extra special to him and hope that I am correct when I say that Rachel held a corner of his heart from the very beginning.

There are so many memories of those years, from the day she started primary school to the day she left to become part of St Mary's College at 11 years of age. Of course there are memories of each of our children growing up, but Rachel was our baby, the child of our later years, and we probably had more time and stability to enjoy her. There had been other babies – one before and twins after she came along – but these three were sadly not to be, so her father and I knew that Rachel was to be our last one. Maybe that was why we made more of her than we would have done in other circumstances.

The fact that Ray had always been away at sea during our other children's formative years made a big difference. In their case, I'd had to manage alone, to be both mother and father to them. It was difficult for them and me, not having a father around to support them, but Rachel was lucky enough to have both of us there from the start. It was certainly easier from my point of view, not having to make all the decisions alone, although there were many times when Mum was considered the villain of the piece. But isn't that usually the case with mothers?

We have always been protective parents, perhaps to a fault. I especially am a born worrier and, because of that, none of our children was allowed to roam at will. Rachel was no exception and, now that her father and I were older and times had changed, we were perhaps overprotective of Rachel. Not once was she allowed to come or go to school unaccompanied, nor was she allowed to play in the street.

Indeed, the area in which we lived did not lend itself to street games, being a main city road with heavy traffic. Added to that, there were very few young children living near by. We got into the habit of inviting Rachel's friends over to our house to play and they would reciprocate. That way we at least had peace of mind and she had company of her own age as often as she wished.

We had a large garden behind the house where Rachel and her brother John spent many hours. There were snowmen and snowball fights in the winter, games of tennis in the summer and all the other things that children like to get up to. Then Rachel acquired a bicycle, which meant rides out to the park with her dad, but never on the roads and never alone. We didn't dare let any of the children do that, so afraid were we of the risk of accidents, having already lost one much cherished family member in a fatal road accident some years previously.

On reflection, I suppose the years we spent in that large house were our happiest. After a long time of uncertainty, when the fishing industry collapsed and we were compelled to leave Hull for Ireland to look for work, we returned. Finally, we were finding our feet again. Rachel reaped the benefits of our renewed security, of having both parents on the scene, and Ray and I had matured enough to perhaps give more of ourselves to her than we had been able to do the others.

Kerry, our eldest daughter, flew the nest early. Having met her future husband, she relocated to the south of England to be nearer to him. Her greatest regret now is that she wasn't around for Rachel's early years, nor indeed for much of the rest of her all-too-short life. Vanda and John were at home with us and John has still not left, so he saw as much of Rachel as anyone, more than the others.

As Rachel grew up, her older siblings had their own lives, which left only Rachel for us to focus our attentions on. And focus we did, simply because we were in a position to do so. It was as if she was our first child. In a way she was, as the first three had never known the pleasure of having their father at home each day. He in turn had not known what it was like to rear a child day in and day out – the joys, the tears and the tantrums, the highs, the lows and all the other little things that parenting involves. I suppose it is also fair to say that, because we were already in our forties, we would normally have been mellowing towards old age. Instead, we had a small girl and felt that we were young again. It was always laughable for me to see the other mothers in the schoolyard when I was delivering or collecting Rachel. The majority of them were only the same age as our eldest daughter and there was I, thinking I was on a par with them! On more than one occasion, both Ray and I were mistaken as her grandparents, so that says it all.

These happy times at St Vincent's, when there was such innocence, are etched in my memory. Rachel, thankfully, was a healthy child and spent very little time off school. She also became involved in extra-curricular activities as soon as she possibly could. Some of the staff and parents had started up a Friday-night club for nine- to 13-year-olds. Her brother John had been a member until he became too old and, as soon as she was able, Rachel also started to attend. This involved walking out in all weathers, as we had done with John. Summer nights were fine, but not so good was turfing out in rain and snow – there for 7pm and back again at 9pm for the return journey. But it was all worth it, as the kids had such a good time and we knew that they were supervised and safe.

During this time we discovered that there was an Irish dancing class in the city. Rachel decided that she wanted to dance, as had her two sisters before her. In fact, I too had danced for many years as a child, so perhaps it was in the blood. She threw herself wholeheartedly into her dancing and it soon became apparent that she had a real flair for it. Even though she appeared on the outside to be quite a shy and reticent child, once she started to perform on stage, she took on a whole new personality.

Classes were on Saturday mornings and some distance away, so travel was not without difficulty. Ray had the family car and was often working at the weekends, so a lot of manoeuvring was called for at times, but we always managed to get there in the end!

I spent many long hours making her costumes – I couldn't do it now because my eyes are not what they were. The hundreds of sequins, the intricate embroidery and the fittings were all a nightmare, but I took great pride in making sure that Rachel's outfits were unique and special. We have lots of photographs from this period – performances at various venues, presentations of awards and memorable St Patrick's Night shindigs at the Irish Centre. It was at this time that Rachel began her lifelong friendship with Saoirse. She became Rachel's dancing partner and was also a school friend. Her mother had taught two of our children at St Mary's College and, being Irish herself, had a lot in common with us. The girls both considered themselves intrinsically Irish, so a strong bond was formed and continued until the day Rachel disappeared. Of course, they made other friends through the years and, after leaving school, Saoirse's life took a different path to Rachel's, but they never lost touch, met up whenever possible and I can safely say that they remained forever friends until the end.

All too soon, it seemed, the time came for primary school to end and for Rachel to move on to her secondary education. Her dad and I couldn't believe how quickly the years had flown by and once again the camera came out, so that Rachel could pose for us in her new uniform. Even though almost every one of her classmates from St Vincent's went on to St Mary's College with her, it was with some trepidation that she set off on her first day. Her father, of course, went to the bus stop with her, and there she met up with a friend who was also a new girl that day. Lesley, too, was a shy girl, the baby of the family, with an equally anxious mother. We must have caused some raised eyebrows between us in the early days, fussing over two very tall girls, both of whom appeared to be much older than they actually were!

It must have been quite a shock for Rachel to leave a small family school where everyone knew everyone else, and to enter a world of hundreds of pupils. It was quite difficult for her at first, being among vast numbers of pupils of all ages and backgrounds, and having to learn many new subjects with many new teachers. It can be said that this is the case for all children, but she had been much more sheltered than most and she was not at all worldly or streetwise at 11 years of age.

It wasn't long before she got into the swing of things. She did very well at her lessons and we received glowing reports from her teachers. She made a lot of new friends who had come to St Mary's from various schools across the city and, naturally, she wanted to catch the bus by herself each day now.

Gradually, she developed other interests apart from her dancing. She was approaching puberty and boys started to figure in her life, as did music. But she still didn't wander far from home and certainly not without us knowing where to and who with. It was still a case of friends coming to our house and she going to theirs, so we all knew where any of them were at any given time. We were lucky that, for the most part, the parents of Rachel's friends were friends of ours and like-minded. This is not to say that we stopped worrying about her. No indeed: if I thought that she was five minutes late coming home from school, I was at the gate looking out for her. This was a habit that prevailed from when the other three children were younger and remains with me to this day.

Some time just before Rachel left primary school, she decided that she wanted to finish her Irish dancing lessons and move on to pastures new. She was desperate to learn ballet and tap dancing, which was my first love, so I enrolled her in classes when she was 11. Having made the arrangements, I took her along one Saturday morning, and I think I was more nervous than Rachel was! There was she, probably one of the tallest in the class, never having done this kind of dancing before, surrounded by all these tiny little girls, many of whom had started to dance before they were three years old. The fact that they were all far more advanced than she was, and, in most cases, much older, did not faze her one bit. She became adept very quickly and in no time caught up with the rest of the class. Ballet was her forte. She was always very slim and graceful and she had perfect feet for the dance, having a very high instep – a trait she shared with my much adored younger brother, Allan, also sadly no longer with us.

Before long she was chosen to do the extra classes that they held for gifted pupils and she had to attend three times a week. Once again, we were traipsing to and fro in all weathers, unless her dad was available with the car. She especially looked forward to the bi-annual dance festivals held locally, when she could compete with other dancers. What excitement there was when she won her first award as a novice! My needlework prowess was required again when it was costume-making time. I still keep all these outfits, together with her ballet, tap and Irish dancing shoes, up in what will forever be Rach's room.

She remained true to her dancing until she was 16. In the later years she spent many of her Saturday mornings helping to train the little ones, a task she really loved, but eventually her interest waned. She became too tall to ever be a ballerina and so became disheartened. Maybe she just didn't have the dedication required. Certainly her feet were always very sore from dancing *en pointe*. She felt that it was all leading nowhere and so, very suddenly, she decided to quit.

She was still at St Mary's, but by now had become friends with a different set of girls. She had sat her GCSEs and gained nine good grades and was now working towards her A-levels. We had once more moved house, and her life had taken on a new dimension. We still insisted on knowing where she was and with whom. She didn't ever really go far but, obviously, she had much more freedom now that she was older. We couldn't always be sure where she was, any more than other parents can, but, although I continued to worry and fear the worst at all times, we had no real concerns about her.

Until this point, Rachel had not seemed to go through adolescence in the same way as her two older sisters had done, around the ages of 13 or 14. In their cases, I was to all intents and purposes a single parent, as Ray was away so much. I had found it hard trying to keep a happy medium, instilling into them the importance of finishing their education, getting a good job, the perils of drink and drugs, and my biggest fear of all – becoming pregnant. There was rebellion naturally and, because their father wasn't there to offer guidance, it was hard going with them at times. However, we managed to rise above it all, and both girls achieved all that I would have wished of them, as did our son, and I expected nothing less of Rachel. In fact, I imagined things would be much easier in her case, because her dad had always been there for her. It was quite a shock to me, therefore, when she seemed to change almost overnight, from being our sweet-natured, pleasing girl to an indifferent, secretive one. Because this didn't happen until she was almost 16, it was even more surprising, although perfectly normal. Looking back, Rachel never did anything untoward, never caused trouble in any sense of the word, but just seemed to lose her direction for a time.

Some time into her A-level courses, she decided she wanted to leave school and go to Hull College instead. This was a great disappointment to me, as all her contemporaries were still at St Mary's and aiming to go to university. This had been my hope for Rachel and, until then, it had been her own ambition too.

Having struggled to make sure our other three children

went on to further education even without their father to encourage them, I was confident that, with both of us around to support her, Rachel would do the same. She had other ideas, however, and I have to admit that I felt let down by Ray in his failure to back me up when trying to get Rachel to reconsider. I felt she was making the wrong decision, while he felt she should do whatever made her happy. Who's to say what the right choice was, but I felt she was leaving school for all the wrong reasons and my opinion has remained unaltered. Rachel had simply decided that she'd had enough of St Mary's but she soon realised that being at Hull College was no different. She had merely swapped one classroom for another, homework and all!

She began a course in IT, plus two other subjects including A-level English, and seemed happy for the most part. She made some nice new friends, though she still kept in touch with her old pals. There wasn't too much socialising out of college hours, as none of the kids had vast amounts of money to spend. In any case, all of them were too young to frequent pubs. Although she had friends of both sexes, she never brought a boy home and there was never any mention of a boyfriend. Mostly she would come home and spend many hours in her room, listening to music and smoking, much to my chagrin. Her room was her domain and she wasn't the tidiest of people, but woe betide me if I dared to enter and clean up! The smoking up there was a particular bone of contention.

Before long, she decided to drop the A-level English to concentrate on IT. She set up her own website and became very adept at the subject. The attraction of being at college soon palled, however, as it was really still the same as school and Rachel wanted something different. I suppose she needed to earn her own money but she wasn't qualified to do a job of any consequence, so what next?

I was still keen for her to work towards qualifying for some profession. Because she had always been interested in cooking and baking, I thought she might change direction and do a catering course. This way, she would be doing practical work but still having day release to the college. She would be trained but would be getting paid to do it.

It was now that she started to work in a hotel and she loved every minute of it, dirty dishes and all. More to the point, the owners, staff and residents all thought very highly of her. I heard such glowing reports of her hard work and willingness to help that I began to wonder if they were talking about the same girl! Pleasant and good-natured she may have been, but willing and hardworking? There must be some mistake! The hoped-for day release never came to pass, however, so the job consisted of her leaving home very early each morning to serve breakfasts. She came home after this but returned to the hotel each afternoon around 5pm to help prepare the evening meal, before finally leaving at 9pm to come home again.

I thought it was very hard on her going out before six each morning, having a fragmented day and then not arriving home until 10pm each night after her evening shift. It wasn't what I had envisaged for her and she was capable of so much more. I felt she was wasting herself there, but I didn't voice these opinions to Rachel as she seemed content and had her own money for the first time. That meant a lot to her and it was certainly easier on our pockets!

She was also deeply into WWF, the American wrestling,

and would rush home each Friday night in order to watch it on TV. Quite often her father or I would pick her up in the car, but otherwise she would travel by bus. As usual, I would stand looking out for her at the time I knew she was due to arrive home. I was always so relieved to see her getting off the bus safely.

She had been at the hotel for about a year when she started to see the light. She realised she would never get her catering qualification, simply because she was never given the time off to attend college. Her only hope was to hang on until the present cook retired, then maybe Rachel would get to take over the job. She decided that she wasn't prepared to wait until that happened and I did not dissuade her. In fact, I was very relieved that she no longer had to go out alone into those dark mornings, when I felt she was more at risk than in the evenings.

Rachel's first thought when she left the hotel was to return to college and this seemed to me a good idea. It never came to pass, though, as things took a very different turn. Our second daughter Vanda had become involved with something, purely by chance and on a voluntary basis. A local entertainer named Johnny Pat, whom we had admired for many years and with whom we'd recently become reacquainted, was about to start a cabaret course for young hopefuls. It was to be run in conjunction with Hull College and involved all aspects of the music industry and cabaret entertainment. Vanda had agreed to help with the administration side and also acted as a chaperone to the students.

Rachel was still unsure of what she wanted to do next, so she decided she would enrol on this course. She enjoyed it greatly and made yet another circle of friends. Johnny Pat taught them a lot about the music business and stagecraft and singing techniques. They also got the opportunity to perform at various venues around the city and were taken away on holiday a few times, to entertain the guests at a holiday camp in Blackpool.

Rachel enjoyed it and learned a lot. It also gave her the chance to use her dancing skills again as she was part of a four-piece group, and she choreographed all their moves. Naturally, there was some falling out amongst the kids, but in the main it was great fun. At the end of the course, all the students achieved a City and Guilds in Cabaret Entertainment, a qualification created especially for this course.

In January 2000, when Rachel was 19, a new intake of students started on the course. Among them was Mark, who was to become her boyfriend, although she didn't know it at the time. He was her first real love, and her last.

Even though Rachel had never been in the habit of gadding about, nightclubbing or going out in general, she always seemed to know a lot of people, but, male or female, they were all just mates to her. As far as I could see, she treated them all the same. Apart from her original school friends, none of them was ever brought home to meet us and we never really knew why. We would have welcomed any of Rachel's friends or acquaintances into our home and she knew this. I can only surmise that she chose to keep her home life and her personal life separate, or perhaps she thought that her friends would not match up to my expectations. I have pondered on this many times since. Did Rachel think that I set standards that she could not uphold? Did I repress her with my constant worrying?

It was important to me that guidelines were given to the

children, especially during the upbringing of the older three because Ray was away so often. In many ways Rachel was privileged in having him there, and I would say that he loved her to a fault. Certainly, we had different attitudes as to how much leeway she ought to be given when she reached an age where she wanted to find her feet. Her happiness was his whole concern, which is not to say that it wasn't mine too – we just had to agree to differ on occasion.

I had already experienced years of rearing children and thought I knew about all their cunning wiles. Being female, I knew exactly what girls were capable of. It was all news to Ray, however, and he wished only that peace and harmony prevailed regardless. It was his first true experience of fatherhood on a daily basis. Every little cough or sneeze Rachel might produce became a full-blown illness in his eyes. This amused me greatly, having nursed the others through every kind of ailment! He totally adored her and she, in turn, was able to twist him around her little finger. Mum, of course, was still the one who existed only to put a spanner in the works. Having said that, I too had experienced only pleasure in her upbringing, apart from those first few whinging years!

I remember her coming home from the cabaret course on Valentine's Day 2000, clutching a card – the first I think she had ever received. She had already mentioned meeting Mark and described him as her 'little friend'. She told me he had bought this card using his bus fare and consequently had to walk all the way home to his village some miles away! It touched her greatly that he would do this for her and this cemented the start of their love affair.

Rachel remained her happy, carefree self while at home, meeting Mark only during the day when on the course.

Neither of them had much money and, as Mark didn't live in Hull, there was little opportunity for them to meet in the evenings. I never imagined it was a serious relationship because, after all, Mark was only 17, almost a year and a half younger than Rachel. When she brought him home for the first time I was quite surprised that he appeared much younger than Rachel. He was also considerably shorter. At 6ft, she found it difficult to find friends her height and she hated the fact she was so tall.

To begin with, I didn't think they were at all suited to each other. Rachel had quite a bubbly personality while Mark was painfully shy. They were like chalk and cheese and at that time I didn't think they had a great deal in common. Obviously, I only saw things from my own viewpoint and the Rachel I perceived was a different character altogether to the one that Mark knew, no doubt. Mark was, and remains, a lovely young man, totally in love with Rachel, and I am sure that he had to put up with a lot from her. I would guess that she was the dominant partner in the equation, though they had both been indulged and were used to getting their own way. We can never know how people are when alone together, but certainly in our presence they seemed very contented with each other.

By now, Rachel's days on the cabaret course were numbered as it only lasted a certain length of time. Apart from a few bits of work, her future was still undecided. Mark was still on the course as he had started after she had, and she continued to go along to support him. They were becoming ever closer but both still lived at their family homes – he in a village outside Hull called Preston and she with us – but there were clouds on the horizon.

When the course ended, Rachel was jobless and penniless. I began to worry that she had lost the plot and her life was heading nowhere. She was a stunning-looking girl with an enviable figure and a good brain. I thought she should be working, earning her own money and meeting other people, enjoying nights out and just doing the things that all young girls do before settling down. There were never any arguments or discussions on the subject, just a certain fraught atmosphere when I put these suggestions to her. Once again, her father and I had to agree to differ and perhaps he was right and I was wrong – who's to say now? Rachel was still very young, still trying to find her niche in society and she had years in which to do so, or so we all thought.

What happened next became the one low point in my relationship with Rachel. I arrived home from work one day to find her in the act of packing up some of her belongings in black plastic sacks. It should not have come as such a shock, as Vanda, who was still helping with the cabaret course and thus saw Rachel and Mark daily, had hinted that Rachel had spoken of moving out. She now wanted to be with Mark all the time and she knew it was not an option in her own home, but it could be if she moved in with him.

I was very upset by this and astounded that she would resort to such a thing without a word to us. I have always shied away from confrontation and I found myself letting her go out of the door without my having uttered a single word. Her father was even more horrified than I was and I still wonder if he didn't hold me responsible in some way for her absconding, because of my pressuring her into finding a job and getting her life back on track. Had I driven her away? The next few months were a very difficult period for us, mainly because Rachel didn't really keep in touch and the only news we had came from Vanda, who she saw constantly and was close to. Indeed, after Vanda had been in hospital, around the time Rachel first met Mark, she stayed at Vanda's for a good many weeks, to help her and look after her. I did see her on a couple of occasions when the kids from the course performed locally.

I couldn't believe that the Rachel we had nurtured and cherished could do this to us without reason. It upset me a great deal, wondering where I had gone wrong. It *had* to be me, as her father had never pressured her. It wasn't that I was worried for her welfare – I knew that Lorraine, Mark's mum, was taking care of her and that she was safe enough in their home. Indeed, there wasn't a lot that they could get up to in far-flung Preston. No, it was just that Rachel had been with us for almost 20 years and now she had suddenly changed her allegiance. I told myself that least said, best mended and bided my time in the hope that she would eventually come around again. I know now that this was the right attitude to take as, after four months or so, she started to make contact again and it was as if that episode in her life had never happened. I suppose she realised that the grass is never really greener on the other side and, after all, there's no place like home!

I knew that, during their time together in Preston, Rachel and Mark had been looking towards getting a place of their own. However, rented and council properties in that neck of the woods were few and far between. Added to which, neither of them was working so money was thin on the ground. So Rachel decided to apply to Hull Council for a tenancy and, within the space of a couple of weeks, she was offered a maisonette on the Orchard Park estate, less than a mile from our house. We had lived in this area on our return from Ireland, but had moved on when Rachel was about three years old. She had a lot of friends on the estate who she had met at senior school and through her dancing, so it was familiar territory to her. Mark was not too keen, as, being from the other side of the city, it was quite alien to him and none of his mates was in that area, but he would have gone to the ends of the earth as long as he was with Rachel.

I was quite dismayed when I first saw the place — it was a tip. It needed a lot of work to put it in order but she was delighted to have somewhere of her own and had many plans and ideas for the decor etc. She was given the keys in January 2001 but they didn't move in for about a month, until carpets were laid, furniture acquired and a certain amount of decorating done. In the event, it never really did get completed the way she wanted it.

We did our best to help, as did Lorraine, and so the day came when they moved in. It was on the upper floor of a two-storey house and even though I had misgivings, I told myself that at least she was near us, which meant that we would still see a lot of her, which we did, and Mark too.

In the beginning, it was all a great adventure to her, as she acted out the role of housewife. Mark had started training to be a painter and decorator and she began work in a creche in the school adjoining our home. She got into the habit of coming along to us after she finished work. She had kept her door key and we never did like to ask her to give it back!

I was still working part-time and now had my own car. The world was our oyster and we travelled far and wide together whenever we could. She would be waiting for me to arrive home in the early afternoon and, more often than not, we would be out and about. This didn't always happen, since I still had my own home to run and two men coming in from work each day expecting to be fed. Rachel, too, in those early days, insisted on having a meal ready for Mark to come home to.

They didn't venture far in the evenings, neither of them being big drinkers or clubbers, and indeed they didn't have the money to do so. They both loved music and Mark in particular was still occasionally performing on the club circuit. He would sometimes visit friends while Rachel liked nothing better than having an early bath and settling down to watch her favourite soap operas. She also indulged her passion for reading. She had a voracious appetite for books and would easily devour one in the time it took Mark to watch one of his videos, which is his personal passion.

Invariably they would both come to us for Sunday lunch but they still spent a lot of time separately with their respective families. It was not at all unusual for Mark to be in Preston while Rachel was here with us. Christmas and the New Year were always spent separately – Mark with his family and Rachel with us. They saw nothing strange in this and neither did we. After all, they were still basically like two small children playing house, with neither of them quite ready to make the final commitment.

I think that these two years, between 2001 and 2003, were my happiest with Rachel. She began to mature and, for me, stopped being a little girl and became my equal. I learned a great deal during that time about what made her tick, and we discussed everything, from cooking to babies, about my Polish father's life during World War II, our time in Ireland and all the other things that only a mother and daughter can share.

She was sorry when her time at the creche ended, as she had made some good friends there and loved the small babies and children. Her hope was to have a family of her own at some stage and she had very fixed ideas about how she would rear them. She thought that she would be strict with them, so obviously the ideas that I had tried to instil in her had not been in vain. I hadn't done everything wrong after all, and I think that in the end Rachel saw her mum as a friend, not just as a cross to bear.

Around this time she obtained employment as a cake decorator. It had been a hobby of mine for years so it was not unfamiliar ground to her, as she had always helped me in the past. Once again, she showed that she had another talent. She enjoyed the work and liked meeting a new set of people. I was concerned because her shift began at 6am and it was a long journey on dark mornings. She got herself a bike, however, and, since there was a cycle track for most of the route, I put my worries aside. She finished work at 2pm so she was still in the habit of coming to us on her way home, though not every day and especially not when the weather was bad.

On a Friday, she would go straight to the pub with some of her workmates and I was pleased that she finally seemed to be enjoying life in the way that most young girls should. She even met up with a few of them some weekends, occasionally by herself but more often than not with Mark. They liked the music scene and Rachel especially loved to dance. I suppose I was a little disappointed that she had set her sights no higher than a cake decorator on a production line. I still thought that she had far more potential than that and, to a point, felt that she was wasting herself and her education, but she herself was happy and that was all that mattered.

She stayed in this job for about eight months, until she left after the Christmas period. It was essentially a seasonal job so the work had started to dry up, and who knows? The early morning starts could have started to pall by then. Mark was still working and Rachel took to spending even more time around at our house during that year. This was the time that I began to get very close to her and we spent many hours together. I'm afraid that Mark's dinner often went uncooked at this stage and the poor lad had to fend for himself! Rachel would have her tea with us, leaving only in time to get home for her beloved *Hollyoaks* and *EastEnders*!

Not once did we let her go off on her own because, even though she had now turned 21, in our eyes she was still our little girl in need of our protection. It was a very short distance from our place to hers, only three or four minutes by car, but we just had to take her home and see her safely in. This was probably more for our own peace of mind than anything else, as Rachel was a great walker and no doubt on occasion would have preferred to make the journey on foot. The only times she didn't get a lift was when Mark was with her, the evenings were light and balmy and they wanted to walk together. Even when Mark was with her, one of us would drop them off more often than not. It was no trouble and we could only relax when we knew they were home safe and sound.

Did we spoil her? To a point, yes, we did and, for her part, she allowed us to indulge her. We had been the same with the others, but more so with Rachel. I suppose that is always the case with the youngest in a family and Rachel was no exception. I know her sisters thought we were over-protective to a fault, that she got far more than they did growing up and continued to do so for much longer. But she was the child of our old age, we were never going to have any more after her, and she kept us so young. Added to that, she was striking and beautiful, turning heads wherever she went. I was very proud that she was my daughter – perhaps too proud, and they do say that pride comes before a fall. How mighty was that fall about to be...

Christmas 2002

Rachel adored Christmas with a childlike excitement and this year was no different. Never normally one to let anything get her down, she was a bit bothered that she wouldn't have much money to spend on presents, as she hadn't had a job for a good few months. I had always helped her out in the past but this time Vanda came to the rescue. She took her into town and paid for all Rachel's gifts to the family – and to Mark. We never let on that we knew this, of course!

As was the norm, she came round about a week before the event and decorated the Christmas tree for us, making sure that everything was just so. I was a bit behind schedule as I was working up until Christmas Eve, finishing at 12.30pm that day. Rachel came to work to meet me and we had a small party: she had helped us to get it all prepared and laid out. After about an hour we left for home. I stopped off to buy a few last-minute presents and we got back to our house mid-afternoon, I to cook and Rachel to relax!

Mark had left for Preston that morning to spend Christmas with his family, which left Rachel on her own. Other years, she had stayed with us during Mark's absence, but this year was different. She had acquired a kitten about three months previously, or so we thought. Unbeknown to me, she had actually got two kittens and she had no intention of leaving them alone overnight.

We enjoyed a happy, busy afternoon until the time came for me to visit some of my relatives to deliver the Christmas cakes I always made for them. Rachel came with me and our final call was to my aunt, who lived very near Rachel. I told her to hop into the car and I would drop her off but she said she would cut across the grass and be at her front door quicker than if I took her. There were security doors at the front and back of her property and she didn't have a key for the back one, which was where the car would take her. Both my aunt and I said she shouldn't do this, as it was after 10pm, very dark and we were concerned for her safety. But she just laughed it off and said she always used that route. We parted having arranged that her dad would pick her up quite early the next morning, Christmas Day, and she would bring her presents for us then.

Ray collected both Rachel and her sister Vanda early on and we spent a quiet but pleasant day, much as other years. Her brother John had bought Rachel and Mark a unicycle as their present, and she thought this very funny. I can see her now in my mind's eye, doubled up in mirth on the floor. She said that she really must get a house with a garden now, so that she could practise riding it. She had wanted to move for some time now, but she kept getting turned down by the council because she had no children.

The next day Rachel came round to us again, having spent Christmas night alone with her kittens. Mark was due back that afternoon, so her dad dropped her off home before nightfall. Even though Ray, John and myself were all back at work between Christmas and the New Year, Rachel still appeared at some stage every day during that week. On Saturday, 29 December, I took her out shopping as there were already a lot of sales on. As usual, bits and pieces caught her eye and, as usual, I indulged her! How ironic that one of the things I bought her that day was a case full of hair accessories – scrunchies in bright colours of red, green and white. When some of her belongings were fished out of the water two weeks later, I was able to identify one of these as hers. It was a green one; I remember it well.

In the days leading up to the holiday period, Rachel had texted John to ask about his plans for New Year's Eve, with a view to joining him and his friends for a night out. This was quite unusual as they rarely went out together and, in fact, Rachel had hardly ever spent New Year anywhere except at home. John had arranged to go to the National pub that night, it being more or less his local, and he told Rachel she was welcome to join him. Mark was also invited but he declined as he didn't know any of their acquaintances and he had no money, and he didn't want John to have to pay for them both all night. Apart from that, Rachel had stayed in to mind the cats over Christmas, so he was more than happy to keep an eye on them at home while Rachel went out and enjoyed herself for a change.

On Tuesday, 31 December, New Year's Eve, both Ray and

myself were at work. John had a day off and so wouldn't be up too early! I left work at 12.30pm and called into a few shops on my way home. I remember looking at the car clock and seeing that it was just after 2pm when I finally set off for home, thinking that I would be back before Rachel arrived. John was upstairs listening to music when I got home and Rachel had not yet appeared. I put my shopping away and then sat for a few minutes to relax.

Very soon afterwards, Rachel came in, full of high spirits and looking forward to the night out. She was wearing her jeans, trainers and a jacket I had bought her as a pre-Christmas present. She was also carrying a large bag containing various items. She had actually brought two dresses with her, as she wanted my opinion on which one I thought she should wear on the night. She had brought a change of clothes for the following day as she was to sleep over in her old room that night and she had a second new jacket with her, one that she'd bought the day before and intended to wear to the pub. It was fake black suede with a fur lining and trim, and she'd considered it a real bargain in the sales. She was absolutely thrilled as it was just her size and she'd used some of her Christmas money to buy it.

She hung around for the rest of the afternoon and I prepared the evening meal. She and John listened to some music and had a bit of banter. Ray arrived home and there was a nice air of excitement around the place. They all had some of the food I had prepared, then around 5.30pm Rachel wanted to start getting ready, as it was to be an early start. As it was New Year's Eve, the pub was expected to fill up quickly and the intention was to get there by 6.30pm. I asked Rachel if she wanted to have a bath, but she said she'd already had one at home and washed her hair.

While John was getting ready to party, Rachel came downstairs in her finery. In the event, she had decided herself which dress to wear and it was one which, although she'd had it for a year, had never worn before. Her friend, Saoirse, had given her a gift voucher for her 21st birthday and Rachel had used it to buy this claret-coloured, sparkly party dress (in a size eight!). It hadn't fitted her then but she had recently slimmed into it and looked a real treat. It had shoestring straps and a handkerchief skirt — quite high-cut on one side but longer on the other. She was also going to wear the new jacket. I told her to be careful not to leave it lying around the pub as it might get stolen, and she replied that she didn't even intend to take it off.

Her hair, which was naturally dark, was quite blonde at this time. She had started with highlights and had gradually got lighter and lighter in the months leading up to December. More often than not, she wore it pinned up, but that night, because of the occasion, she wore it loose and it hung past her shoulders. I remarked on how light it was now and she told me that she intended to dye it back to its natural colour in the New Year. She normally wore a lot of jewellery, but that night she wore only a pair of gold hoops in her ears, a gold clown on a chain that Mark had given her for Christmas, and a gold crucifix round her neck. She had left her watch in her room upstairs along with all her other things.

Just before they left, John had a phone call and shouted out to ask me if I was willing to babysit for a couple of his friends who wanted to join them in the pub. I had never met the child and I was rather tired, but I didn't want to seem mean so I agreed. It would only be for a few hours and I had no other plans for that night. Ray and I are invited every year to our next door neighbour's house for their annual New Year's Eve party, but we had decided not to go this year, as we were both feeling the after-effects of Christmas and were tired.

John went off in his car at around 6.30pm to pick up a few of his pals and drop them at Steve and Sandy's, where I would later be babysitting. The plan was for everyone to congregate there and then walk the short distance to the pub. While Rachel was waiting for John to come back, she, for the first time in her life, asked her dad if he would lend her some money. She had never had to ask, as Ray always offered it voluntarily! As he was short, he went out to the nearest cash point and got her what she had asked for, which was only £10. She never spent it that night, but it was never found either.

John and Rachel said they would walk up to Steve and Sandy's but Ray was having none of it and insisted on driving them, a distance of a quarter of a mile at the most! On his return, we sat around until it was time for him to drop me off for my babysitting duties at around 8pm. I had agreed to watch the child until around 10.45pm, at which time Ray would pick me up and take me home. I know that I was a little apprehensive at meeting their child, Alfie, for the first time, as his reputation preceded him! He was five years old and very precocious but I enjoyed being with him for those few hours. His parents arrived back at the appointed hour and I rang Ray to ask him to collect me. I hadn't driven myself as parking was a problem near their house but I didn't want to be out too late, as Ray had been up since 4am and would be very tired by now.

Unbeknown to John and Rachel, it was fancy dress in the pub that night and the couple for whom I was babysitting had gone all out – he dressed as Austin Powers and she as Liz

Hurley. They had won a bottle of champagne for their efforts and were very happy when they got home. I asked especially if Rachel was enjoying herself when they left and they said she was. The whole crowd of them were to see in the New Year at the pub and then call in at Steve and Sandy's on their way home, to celebrate with them for a time. I chatted with them until Ray arrived but we didn't linger, as I just wanted to get home. It had been a long day, especially for Ray.

As soon as I got in, I went up and had a bath and changed into my nightclothes. We are not a couple who normally go out socially, but we are in the habit of having a few drinks most nights and this night was no exception. Ray had a couple of vodkas while I was in the bath and normally I would have joined him. However, because I had eaten practically nothing all day, I decided that vodka on an empty stomach might not be a good idea! Instead, I had a glass of Bailey's Irish Cream, by which time it was around midnight. We saw in the New Year and then went into the back garden to watch the fireworks being set off all around us. By now, the party next door was in full swing and, judging by the noise, they were all having a good time.

We went back inside and I rang Kerry, our oldest daughter, in Southampton to wish her a Happy New Year. As usual when the two of us start talking, the conversation went on for longer than anticipated and it was more than half an hour later when I put the phone down. Ray, who had been hovering around and waiting to go to bed, called out his greeting to Kerry and then went upstairs at exactly 12.40am.

I didn't expect to see John and Rachel for quite some time and thought I would be long asleep before they came home. I decided to have a final glass of Bailey's and then retire to bed, but instead I picked up a book and started reading. I lost track of time so it was quite a surprise when I heard the door being unlocked and the two of them bounded into the room. It was only 1.20am.

They were both in good spirits and John was very merry, having had quite a few drinks. He went upstairs at once and came down soon after, all ready for bed. Rachel chatted for a while and said she'd had a good time although she'd drunk very little, only a few glasses of lager. She was keen to get to bed herself but said she would first ring Mark and used the phone in the kitchen to do so. It soon became apparent that Mark was not at home as Rachel had expected. He'd received a last-minute invitation to a party, which was where he was when she reached him on his mobile. Rachel became very upset when she realised he'd left the kittens alone at home and said so in no uncertain terms. John and I were quite bemused by it all and John went up to bed laughing. I didn't see it as a big deal either, as the kittens were inside, could come to no harm and would not starve overnight!

Rachel sat in the kitchen and lit up a cigarette while I stayed in the back lounge. There is an obscure glazed window between these two rooms and through it I could see her outline quite clearly. I was waiting for her to finish her cigarette and go to bed, so that I could do so as well.

I suppose I must have been dozing off when I heard the back door closing, as her words didn't register at all and, by the time I had roused myself, I heard her unlock the door and come back in again. She went upstairs and I was relieved that she had decided to stay and go up to bed after all. Instead, she came back downstairs, having changed from her strappy evening shoes into her trainers. I realised afterwards that this was why she had gone out and then returned – she didn't want to make the journey home in high heels. She moved towards the door again and this time I jumped up and went after her.

By now it was around 1.45am on a very cold and windy night and I was worried about her intentions, but she said she was going home to her own place. I followed her outside on to our drive and tried to reason with her, begging her not to go, but she was adamant. At one point I looked at our cars with the idea of driving her home, but, having had a few drinks, I knew there would be a risk if I were to be stopped by the police. I said this to Rachel and she said it didn't matter, as it wasn't far and she would be OK. She would telephone me when she arrived home anyway.

I followed her a little way along the street, still very worried and asking her to reconsider. She became quite irritated with me for making a fuss and said that she must go home as the kittens were alone in the dark and would be hungry. I tried all kinds of arguments to make her stay, the final one being that her father would kill me when he found out I had let her go on her own at that hour, but it was to no avail. She was determined to go.

Even though it was New Year's Eve, the road was strangely deserted, but there was one person around. A young man was approaching as we went out of the driveway. He drew level with us during my final conversation with Rachel and so must have heard much of what was said. At one point, I was so desperate that I considered shouting after him and asking if he would walk her home, but then I realised how unwise that would be. He was a stranger and in any case, when I looked up, he seemed to have disappeared. I had to force myself to get a grip and stop worrying – Rachel was almost 22 years old, a fit girl, well used to walking distances and, after all, it was only about three-quarters of a mile home along a busy, well-lit road. On top of that, it was New Year's Eve when all the world was happy and enjoying itself. I was just being a stupid mother and Rachel's final words to me were, 'I'll be OK, don't worry,' and that she would ring when she got home. What was to happen next was a nightmare from which we will never wake up, and one from which we will never, ever recover.

Wednesday, 1 January 2003

At 2.20am Rachel had been gone for about 20 minutes. I guessed it would take her roughly this long to reach home, maybe a little longer, given that it was a windy night. I knew that, having promised to ring me, she would do so and would not keep me up all night waiting for her call. However, being the worrier that I am, and knowing that I wouldn't rest until I knew she was safely home, I decided to ring her first. I waited until about 2.25am and then tried her home number but there was no reply. I figured she had not yet reached her house and so tried her mobile but this too went unanswered. I thought this was strange. Where was Rachel? Had I miscalculated how long it would take her to get home, or had she arrived and gone straight to bed? I was sure she must have heard one of her phones ringing in any case, and would have had no reason not to answer my call. I tried reaching her again about ten minutes later, first on her landline and then on her mobile, and continued to do so at similar intervals throughout the night. She never answered.

By now I was seriously worried and did not know what to think or, indeed, what to do. I considered waking her dad and brother, but, having had the amount of drink that we'd had, none of us could safely go out in the cars to search for Rachel. And where would we look in any case? She was obviously not at home. I decided she must have gone looking for Mark, who she knew was at a party some five miles away. That was the only explanation I could come up with, so at around 4.30am I stopped trying to reach her and reluctantly went up to bed, despite the terrible feeling of foreboding which enveloped me.

The next morning I didn't wake up until about 10am, having been up most of the night. I heard Ray on the telephone and dashed downstairs, thinking it would be Rachel. However, it was Vanda, ringing to wish us a Happy New Year. I took the receiver from Ray and gave her a brief resume of what had happened during the night. Ray was horrified when he heard this, as he thought Rachel was still asleep upstairs and his panic set in immediately. We started to ring Rachel's two telephones at once. Her landline went unanswered and now we were unable to connect with her mobile. Vanda began sending texts and Ray decided to drive round to Rachel's flat to see if she was there after all. He had already started to cook a large joint of beef which we had bought for the occasion and had prepared all the vegetables to accompany it. In the event, we never got round to eating it, and the whole lot was consigned to the bin the next day.

Ray returned from the flat, having been unable to gain entry, though he said he thought he could hear movement inside. I continued to telephone, becoming increasingly worried as I still got no answer. John came down and, when we told him what had happened, he too, began calling on his mobile. At once he got an engaged signal from her house number. We were so relieved. Someone must be in the flat. Rachel must have found Mark during the night and they had both just got home. I rang again and the phone was answered – thank God! However, it was Mark who picked up the phone. My heart sank. When I asked him if Rachel was there, he replied no – she was staying with us, wasn't she? He went on to say that he had only arrived home from his friend's house at 7am, wet through with rain. He had ridden home on Rachel's bike and didn't think that she had been home at all, as everything looked as it had when he had left the night before. The cats, he was sure, hadn't been fed and there was no sign of Rachel, or any of the clothes she'd been wearing.

On hearing this, Ray, John and myself became panicky. Our only hope now was that Rachel had decided to spend the night with one of my relatives who live locally. The other alternatives were a couple of her old school friends, though I didn't think it likely that she would be at any of these places. We went through the motions anyway, only to find that, as we'd suspected, none of them had seen her. The only thing now was to report her disappearance to the police, even though it was just 12 hours since she had last been seen. This task fell to John and I, since, by now, Ray had started to fall apart.

On the way to the police station, we called in at the flat to see Mark and to tell him our intention. I went up alone, while John kept the engine of his car running. Even then, I had to make quite sure Rachel wasn't there. Mark said afterwards that he thought I was jumping the gun by going to the police so soon. Rachel knew loads of people and could be anywhere. I, her mother, knew that she would not just walk out and stay out of touch. It was totally out of character and there was no reason on earth why she should do so. She had left me on good terms with the intention of getting home to the kittens as soon as possible. Somewhere along the way she had vanished.

As it was New Year's Day there was only a skeleton staff on duty at the police station, but we gave them our statement. After about 20 minutes, another two officers arrived and questioned us further about Rachel. They decided to visit the flat and check things out for themselves. John and I followed, picking up Vanda along the way. We arrived to find the flat upside down and Mark, having realised the seriousness of the situation, in a very upset state. There was no sign of Rachel, nothing to say she had been back to the flat and nothing that we could do about it.

We went home, leaving Mark with his mother who had driven in from Preston, and spent a very worrying evening, going over things time and again and wondering what could have happened. John and Ray went out searching far and wide, with neither of them really knowing where to look. It grieves me greatly to know they both walked past where she was eventually found, as did Mark, while searching endlessly over the next four weeks. She was so near but we didn't know it. It is strange, though, that, during the very early days of her disappearance, when Vanda asked Mark what he thought had happened, he said he felt she was still very near. I spent the night sitting up alone with Rachel's old cat, Tom, while the men managed to snatch a few hours' sleep.

The next day, Wednesday, 2 January, dawned and we'd

heard nothing from the police, so Ray and Vanda decided to go to the station. Unfortunately, all the computers were down, a new set of staff were on duty and Ray thought they seemed unconcerned about Rachel's disappearance. This turned out not to be true, but it was still early days and, as they pointed out, she was almost 22 years old. They were still, however, treating her disappearance seriously and that afternoon a detective arrived at our door to take further statements. I took to him at once and, in fact, it was partly due to his vigilance that Rachel was eventually found, so we thank you, Tony.

Our detective was quite inexperienced in this field, however. He had never been involved in a missing-person case before, so, when Rachel did not turn up after a day or so, the case was passed on to those in higher authority. We were assigned two family liaison officers, Steve and Ian, who were both towers of strength to us in the very dark days ahead. We were told from the outset that these were 'real' coppers and were not there just to offer tea and sympathy. Over the weeks that followed, we got to look forward to their twice-daily visits and we talked about anything and everything. They kept us going through the bad times, as did their colleague, Kay.

Throughout those first terrible days, Ray shut himself away alone in a room and I didn't know how to help him. He cried continuously for almost two weeks and I became very concerned for his physical wellbeing. He was unable to face anyone, wouldn't speak to the police or answer the telephone, and was unwilling to involve himself in dealing with the media. That task fell to John and I, though it was the last thing that either one of us wanted, or had imagined that we would ever have to do. In my desperation, I threatened to call the doctor out to Ray, but, in the end, I called our old friend and one-time parish priest, Father White. He came at once and, though he, too, was unable to console Ray, he continued to visit us every day, sometimes twice a day, from then until long after Rachel's funeral. Rachel's death and the manner of it has affected him profoundly.

The days that followed will remain in my memory forever and haunt my dreams every night. To begin with, we didn't alert our oldest daughter Kerry about Rachel's disappearance, thinking it unfair to burden her with what might be nothing of any great consequence. For the same reason, we didn't tell any of Ray's family living in Ireland, or any of our other relatives scattered around the globe. On the Friday, however, the police suggested we let everyone know, as there would now be a lot of media coverage. It was best that they heard it from us rather than saw it on the television or read it in the newspaper.

Everyone was greatly shocked, terribly worried and Kerry drove up immediately from her home in Southampton to be with us and offer support. She had to leave her husband, who was recovering from heart surgery, and her three young children, the youngest of whom is severely autistic, but she was very positive when she arrived late that evening. Afterwards, she admitted that she, too, had feared the worst, but at the time she did her best to make us all feel better, saying that Rachel must have gone off on her own accord and of course she would return safe and well. She made the journey again the following weekend in atrocious weather and we missed her desperately each time she left.

Press releases began to go out and interviews for both radio and television were called for. Ray was initially unable to attend any of these, so I, who normally shied away from even having my photograph taken, found myself very much in the public eye, together with John. There was no time to worry about it – it had to be done and I seemed to exist on autopilot from day to day. I hardly slept and none of us ate enough to feed a sparrow. It was as if we were on the outside looking in on a scene that didn't concern us. It was surreal. Even seeing Rachel's face on national television, reading about her in the newspapers and hearing her name spoken didn't make it any more real. It all went over our heads because it didn't seem possible that it was our Rachel they were talking about. There had to be some mistake.

Those first two weeks passed by in a whirl of interviews, press conferences and the daily visits by the police. They had to look into every aspect of Rachel's life and background to find out if there was any reason at all for her to disappear so abruptly. They drew a blank, but it was still very upsetting for us, her family, not to mention poor Mark, her boyfriend, who was absolutely devastated. Lots of fingers were pointed at him, but we maintained from the start that he would never harm Rachel. It was very difficult to try and comfort him, as we had no comfort to give. We ourselves were shattered, distraught, and each of us knew in our hearts that something terrible had happened to her.

It was particularly stressful to know that rivers and drains were now being dragged, and that fields and gardens in the vicinity of Rachel's flat were being searched. The flat was taken apart by police teams on three separate occasions, another body blow to Mark, though necessary at the time. He continued to stay at the flat, barely sleeping and constantly searching the area day and night, looking for her endlessly.

We were assured by the police that she was still just a missing person, since no evidence to the contrary had come to light. We all continued to torment ourselves by trying to conjure up scenarios, from accidents to her leaving town for pastures new. At the end of the day though, I think each one of us knew the truth, but, by some tacit agreement, we never voiced our fears aloud.

On 17 January, Rachel's 22nd birthday, the police put a tap on our telephone, just in case she tried to get in touch on that day. It came and went without a word, as I had known it would. I had been without hope since day one, but my fears were compounded now and there was little point in pretending any more.

Then came Saturday, 19 January, two days after her birthday. I was on the phone to Ray's cousin in Australia when I looked up to see Steve, one of our liaison officers, coming to our door in a hurry. I was afraid, because it was unusual for them to turn up without telephoning us first, so it was not a good sign. I asked immediately if it was bad news and Steve made a rocking motion with his hand. He then told us that some of Rachel's belongings had been fished out of a drain about a mile from her home. These items included her mobile phone, Irish passport and some other items. A trainer was also among the things recovered. We were shown photographs and were able to identify them as hers, though we were not allowed to see the actual items.

Things were now looking extremely grim, yet we still tried to cling to some small hope when really there was none. During this time, we received many cards and messages of support from friends old and new, as well as others from those we didn't even know. They came not just from our own city but from around the country and, indeed, the world. I believe these messages and the prayers of others helped keep me going throughout those days. I certainly couldn't even begin to pray, but Ray never ceased to during that terrible period.

Ray and I, together with Vanda and John, gave one final press conference, which was very harrowing for us all. Mark could not bring himself to attend. He is a very shy and introverted person at the best of times and by now he was in a dreadful state, barely eating or sleeping. We begged anyone with a conscience or a heart to come forward and speak to the police if they knew anything about Rachel and naturally there were plenty who thought that they did. There were supposed sightings of her all over the town and even further afield but they turned out in the main to be unfounded. Particularly worrying were the so-called sightings around the area where Mark had been on New Year's Eve, and we began to wonder if she had fallen into the treacherous river Hull near by.

We nearly drove ourselves mad with our theories and before long ended up at each other's throats. There seemed to be so many possibilities and none of them was good.

Towards the end of January, the police told us that they were going to offer an amnesty to anyone who might be able to shed any light on Rachel's disappearance. They would overlook any petty crimes if anyone came forward with information that would help to solve the mystery. This was duly printed in the papers.

The liaison officers were in the habit of ringing us each morning after their daily police briefing to tell us they were on their way. On 27 January, however, they told us beforehand they would be at the house at 8.30am the next morning. They usually came at least an hour later than this, so it seemed rather strange. Also odd was the fact they had told us of this the day before. We had a bad feeling and wondered if something was afoot.

Early the next morning, Lisa, the police press officer, arrived first and gave us a statement to read. This said that the police intended to search all houses within a mile of Rachel's flat, about 300 houses in all, and this would involve 100 officers. Lisa said that this statement would go out to the media at 9am and, in the meantime, we should not divulge this information to anyone. Who would we tell in the space of half an hour? I wondered. Apart from our children, we have very few relatives in Hull.

Our two liaison officers arrived soon afterwards to reiterate what Lisa had said but after a short time they all left, saying they would come back later. I don't know what we thought of it all, but for sure there was a certain atmosphere around – fear, trepidation, a feeling that something was about to happen. We watched the television for a while and saw scenes of police officers entering people's homes to search them and the residents' comments. We wondered what the police had in mind and what they hoped to achieve by this. Did they know something that they weren't telling us?

Around midday, Ian rang to tell us that the search was going well and the locals were being very co-operative. He then asked us if we would be willing to go on regional television to thank the local people for their continuing help in all of this and of course we agreed. We needed the public's support and it was the least we could do. We would have done anything if it meant finding Rachel.

It was arranged that the television crew would arrive at our house at about 2pm. Lisa would be with us before then and both our liaison officers would be in attendance. Feeling very nervous, we ate nothing. Lisa arrived at 1.30pm and said the television crew would be arriving very soon to set things up. We waited for Steve and Ian to get to the house. I had made some small effort to tidy myself up and had put on a bit of makeup for the television appearance. By 1.50pm there was still no sign of the two officers. We were getting quite worried, and Lisa too, we could sense, did not seem quite herself.

Suddenly Steve and Ian burst in and the air was electric. They said that the television interview was to be called off immediately because something had happened, and the boss, Detective Superintendent Paul Davison, was at the scene even as they spoke. Lisa was in a quandary as the television crew were about to knock on our door and it was down to her to put them off with no explanation. I didn't envy her but, at the same time, was filled with terror. Obviously, something serious had occurred but I couldn't imagine what.

Lisa must have been able to forestall the television people, as I didn't see any sign of them. I don't recall seeing her leave, but, with John upstairs and Ray elsewhere in the house, it was just Ian, Steve and myself who sat waiting, for what I didn't quite know. I do know that both of them seemed very agitated, glancing furtively at each other and at me, and it felt like the balloon was going to go up at any minute. I really don't know what I expected or what was in my mind right then, except fear.

This peculiar uneasiness between the three of us lasted five or ten minutes, until I said I wasn't prepared for the three of us to sit looking at each other any longer and asked if either of them would like a cup of tea. For the first time ever, Ian replied that he would make me one. I realised then that they must know something, as they both knew I never drank tea or coffee. Maybe I would need a cup now is what must have been in their minds. As it happened, it was me who made the tea for them, which they sat drinking in a nervous manner. Neither Ray nor John had made an appearance by this stage, and for me it felt as if time was standing still.

At length, Ian said that he was waiting for DS Davison to ring him with some information but, if he hadn't done so in the next 20 minutes, Ian would call him. No sooner were these words out of his mouth than his mobile rang and a short conversation ensued, the content of which I didn't hear, not that it would have made much sense to me anyway.

Looking very anxious, Ian now said that Paul Davison wanted to have a few words with him in private, so he went outside for the remainder of the call. Steve and I went into the kitchen. Steve had an agitated manner about him and looked very concerned. By now, Ray had joined us and John was just coming down the stairs. Then Ian came back into the house and his next words are engraved on my memory: 'Oh, you're all three here together. Well, there is no easy way to say this. We have found a body and two men have been arrested on suspicion of murder. I'm very sorry ...'

So it was Ian, the quieter and less brash of the two officers, who had drawn the short straw, but they had obviously both known of this before they'd arrived that day. Rachel had actually been found at around 1pm and by now it was 2.30pm.

Suddenly everything fell into place. Now it had happened — the news we had been dreading yet expecting for the last four weeks had become a terrible reality. Rachel, our beautiful

Rachel, our baby, was dead, murdered, and had been lying mere yards from the home she shared with Mark, all those weeks. Stunned and disbelieving, the three of us just stood huddled together and the only one of us who broke down momentarily was John. Until now, he had been the only one of us who had refused to face up to the fact that some awful fate had befallen her but now he had to accept it.

For some reason, I felt a sense of relief as well as a great sorrow. I had known, with a mother's instinct, that Rachel was gone. Even from New Year's Eve I had known that there would be no happy ending for us, all the while willing her to be found. I knew that I could not go through the rest of my life wondering if she was out there somewhere. Now, at least, we would get her back, be able to put her to rest, and the perpetrator of this heinous crime had been apprehended. It was no consolation but we were luckier than some parents who find themselves in similar situations.

Ian and Steve tactfully left the three of us alone for a short time before getting down to brass tacks. There were practical things to be done, not the least being that our families needed to be told what had happened before the media got hold of the story. Mark, too, had to be told and his liaison officers were imparting the grim news to him even as we spoke. I didn't dare to think how he would take it but I knew that Lorraine, his mother, was with him for support, as she had been throughout his ordeal.

We telephoned as many people as we could and then Vanda was brought to the house by Ian and Steve. We hadn't wanted to tell her the dreadful news over the phone and so they had gone and told her for us. None of us had much to say to each other, for what was there to say? Our worst fears had been confirmed. This was a living nightmare that none of us could comprehend. We were in complete and utter shock.

Of the two people arrested that day, only one was eventually charged with Rachel's murder, the other being released on police bail after 72 hours. At that point, we knew only the address where she had been found, not the manner in which she had died. The horrendous details of that came later.

For now, we just knew that Rachel was still at the scene of crime, awaiting the arrival of the pathologist and would be moved later that evening. I couldn't bring myself to watch the television coverage, to see the place where Rachel was still lying and all the onlookers gathering there. I only knew that my precious girl was less than a mile away and that we, her family, could not go to her. I don't know how Mark stayed in the flat all this time, knowing she was only yards away from him, but he could not be budged – he just needed to be near her, he said. She was no longer ours – she belonged to the state now, to the police and the pathologist who would soon have to desecrate her poor body even more to perform the post mortem. I also knew that the next day Steve and Ian would return to divulge the cause of death. I slept not a wink that night.

The next morning, Ray and I were up very early. I was in the kitchen while he was in the television lounge. It had become his habit, while Rachel was missing, to scan the TV for any news. I considered this a form of self-torture and never watched it. He had already collected Vanda, so she too was at the house. Suddenly we heard the most dreadful cries from him. He had seen the reports about Rachel and I learned afterwards that they said she had suffered 'a violent and sustained attack' and a 'traumatic death'. His grief was heartbreaking and frightening to behold. He was like someone possessed, running through the house, crying and shouting, punching doors and walls, saying over and over, 'My poor girl, my poor girl.' I didn't ask what he had seen and I didn't try to comfort him, as there was no point. There was no comfort.

When Ian and Steve arrived later on, I went off into another room, as I couldn't face what they had to say. Vanda did feel a need to know how Rachel had died and it was from her that I later learned she had died from stab wounds. At this stage, that is all that was revealed, not the severity or anything else. In fact, we were to learn the details from a different source entirely. Ray and I did not ask, preferring to shut our minds to how much our beautiful girl must have suffered.

We spent the next day in a state of high tension. The police had 72 hours to question both suspects and could then apply for an extension if necessary. When we were told that one of them had been released on bail, we became very worried. Our fears were thankfully unfounded and, just before the allotted time expired, one man was charged with her murder. It came as a great relief to hear this, though we were all still fearful as to whether the charge would stick.

Rachel had been found on Tuesday, 28 January, four weeks to the day since she had gone missing. Her alleged murderer was charged on Thursday the 30th and was summoned to appear in court the next morning. By this time Kerry had driven up from Southampton and it was she who accompanied Ray to the court that day. At that point, the alleged murderer was of no consequence to me; it was enough for me to know that Rachel had gone and there was little doubt in anyone's mind that he was the culprit.

The headlines screamed out, FACE TO FACE WITH A KILLER and the media went to town on the story. It was heartbreaking to see pictures of Ray and Kerry, both on the television and in the newspapers, trying their best to remain dignified through it all. They were reading the statement we had composed together the night before, but both of them, I knew, were destroyed inside. In Ray's case, he was on the point of collapse. They were both shocked when they saw Rachel's alleged murderer. The person we had been told was 22 years old, almost exactly her age, was not the youth we all had imagined. Instead, they saw a man, a stocky, powerfully built individual, not as tall as Rachel but heavily tattooed, bearded and looking at least ten years older than his supposed age. His name was Michael Little.

We had imagined that Rachel, being a very fit and athletic girl, would have been able to fend off any attacker, or at least run away. When Ray and Kerry saw this character, however, they knew at once that Rachel would not have stood a chance against him. He spoke only to confirm his name and was remanded in custody to reappear a week later.

On this occasion, John and Vanda went along with Ray. Mark too attended, as did our old friend Father White. I still did not need to have sight of this individual. Mark, having been shown his photograph, wanted to be absolutely sure he had never set eyes on him before. This turned out to be a fact — Mark had not seen him before, not even around the neighbourhood, even though their homes were only yards from each other. He was a stranger to Mark and, almost certainly, to Rachel too. A random killing and thus the rarest of all. He had moved into the area only a couple of months earlier, so he could not have known Rachel or anything about her. She had just been in the wrong place at the wrong time, we were told.

That day he was remanded once more to appear for a plea and directions hearing at a date some months ahead. Our shattered family returned home to face up to the terrible days that lay ahead. Such things as the opening and adjournment of the inquest into Rachel's death, the release of her body and finally the unthinkable – arranging her funeral. Little did we think when we saw her so happy and carefree on New Year's Eve, so healthy and full of life, that we would be burying her body two months later. The most awful irony of it all were her last words to Ray that night, which were, 'I think 2003 is going to be my year ...' Well, now it certainly was but not in a way that she, or we, could have predicted.

We had a lot of support, both during Rachel's disappearance and after she was found. This came in the form of letters, cards, flowers and hundreds of messages of sympathy. They came from all over the world and eventually numbered about 500. The local people were shocked, upset and even ashamed that such an event could have occurred in their neighbourhood. We were comforted by the knowledge that the perpetrator of this crime was not a local and that Rachel's faith in her fellow neighbours was, in the end, justified.

The date of Rachel's funeral was set for 28 February, exactly one month from the day she had been found. That month flew by in a flurry of activity. Father White continued to visit us every day to offer solace, as he had done throughout, and there was still a lot of police presence – their work was just beginning. But apart from a couple of flying visits from various members of Ray's family, we were very much alone. This may seem surprising, but, in general, friends and neighbours stayed away, not really knowing what to say or do, though my own few relatives were there for us.

Then came one particularly bad morning when Rachel's interim death certificate dropped through our letterbox and was opened by Ray. Until then, because he was in such a bad way, we had refrained from discussing her injuries. I didn't think he could cope with it. He was very quiet and I asked him what had been written as her cause of death, to which he replied, 'Multiple stab wounds to the neck and chest.' This had not been made public. though I myself had already learned of it – even down to the number of wounds. I had tried to keep it from Ray, but now he too knew and it was a terrific blow to him. Probably the most upsetting part was that the date of death was given as 28 January, when we knew it had occurred on the first of the month. This, however, is the law. It was the date on which she was found and when the post mortem took place and must forever remain so. To us, though, she will always be remembered from 17-1-81 to 1-1-03.

Friday, 28 February 2003

Rachel's funeral was as wonderful an occasion as it could be, given the circumstances surrounding it. Many hundreds of people attended: relatives, friends and parishioners, along with work colleagues of Ray, John and myself, not to mention the police contingent and of course the media. Sixteen of Ray's family members made the journey from Ireland and I think we did her proud. Father White played a very large part in it all, even arranging for us to have use of St Vincent's club afterwards, where a lovely buffet had been prepared. It wasn't really sad – it all went over our heads simply because none of us could still believe what had happened.

We had a burial as opposed to a cremation, as that is what Rachel would have wanted. She had a lifelong fear of fire and Mark was especially anxious that she should not be burned because of it. It gave us great comfort to know so many people had known and loved Rachel and that they had wanted to come and pay their respects, to say goodbye. Words can't describe, however, our sorrow when we saw our beloved daughter's coffin being lowered into the ground on that cold, dank Friday morning. We hadn't even been able to see her one last time, to touch her or kiss her. She had been identified by DNA methods only and that was one of the hardest things to bear. There had been no finality to it and, in some irrational moments, we still ask ourselves if it is really her lying in that cold, lonely grave.

It was a very low point two days later when all the family had to return to their own homes. They had kept us buoyant for a time but that time was now over and the stark reality hit us — we were alone. Rachel was gone forever. She was never coming back and this was to be our lives from now on.

How, then, will we ever come to terms with her loss? How can we even begin to understand why this terrible nightmare should have befallen us, an ordinary family, in an ordinary street, in an ordinary town? How could this happen to a girl like Rachel? Above all, how will she be remembered in the future?

I would never try to place her on a pedestal. She was neither saint nor sinner, but just your average girl-next-door. She was happy-go-lucky and didn't really let things get her down. She loved children and animals; she was clever and kind and she was beautiful, but it isn't just because I'm her mother I say that — everybody said it.

Of course she had her moments — who doesn't? But in her case, they were very few and far between, and in the main so trivial they hardly bear mentioning. She was certainly on the side of the underdog and no matter the colour or creed: in her eyes everyone was equal. If there was anyone she didn't like, that person would never be aware of it because she hid her feelings very well. In fact, she smiled her way through life and it was ever a pleasure to have her around.

I have so many memories of Rach, from childhood to adulthood, that I would hardly know where to begin, but some are more special than others. The day of her first Holy Communion was one of them. She looked like a miniature bride in the white dress and veil I had made for her. She was so innocent and so excited to have all her family there to celebrate the occasion with her. That was probably the first time I had been glad I'd had a daughter instead of the second son I had been longing for. The boys didn't look half as good in their outfits! By contrast, her baptism hadn't been anything like as pleasurable as this day because she had cried her way through that and it turned into a fiasco!

Another wonderful day was when she reached the final of The Face Of Hull 1999, against great opposition. She didn't win on that occasion but we were very proud that she got that far. It didn't bother her one jot being a runner-up – she just went all out to enjoy herself and was thrilled with what she did achieve.

There were times when she, in the pursuit of pleasure, left us behind feeling sad and worried. The time we let her fly alone to Ireland to spend the summer with her cousin. Full of fear, Ray and I drove her to the airport, she delighted to be going while I was in tears the moment she boarded the plane! It was no different when, a couple of years later, she went off to America for a holiday without us. I knew she would be perfectly safe with Kerry and her family, but it didn't stop us driving ourselves mad for the duration of her stay. The photographs she brought back were hilarious, with Rachel so sunburned she looked like a Red Indian! We'll treasure them always, together with every other picture and video we have of her.

I recall the many miles we walked together, the shopping trips, the rummaging through charity shops to find books and the long discussions we had in later years. The happy family holidays spent in Ireland, the land of her birth, and her tears every time we had to leave for home. A very memorable journey by car across Europe to visit some of my family in Poland. Above all, I remember her good nature at all times, even when the last thing she wanted to do was humour me. Whenever I showed her things that were probably of no interest to her whatsoever, we got her stock phrase, 'That's rail [sic] nice!' I can hear her even now and her perfume will linger forever.

But the most haunting memory I have is that of the last time I saw her. She was walking away from me on New Year's Eve and I never even saw her face. I had to share this memory with the rest of the country since this is the image that was captured on the CCTV and shown on the television news and pictured in the newspapers for the world to see. It will never be erased from my mind and will live with me forever.

The beast that murdered Rachel, the one who committed this most heinous of crimes, can have no idea of how he has destroyed not just me, her mother, but her entire family and all who loved her. This is an ongoing tale. Each of us is still struggling to cope with the situation. This is his legacy to us.

Her father is a broken man, a man who grew old before my very eyes in the space of five months. He will never recover.

Her two sisters, one of whom might have had a new lease of life had Rachel lived. Vanda, a chronically sick girl for more than 20 years, is in desperate need of a kidney transplant and Rachel may well have been the one person in the family who could and would have helped her. Although there was an age gap of 12 years, they were very close and not just sisters but best friends. Her older sister, Kerry, who never knew her as well as the rest of us, and now never will.

Her only brother, John, the nearest in age to Rachel. He was with her on the night she disappeared and is wracked with guilt because he went to bed instead of walking her home. How could he possibly know what was to happen? He will never get over this.

Then there is Mark, her first love, her sweetheart, who feels that his life is over at only 21 years of age. He, too, is riddled with guilt that he decided to go out that night instead of staying home with their kittens. If he'd been there when she called, she would almost certainly have stayed with us overnight. But he was entitled to go out that night, just as Rachel was entitled to walk home unaccosted.

There are the cousins in Ireland, one of whom has had recurring nightmares since Rachel went missing. She, too, has her memories, as have every one of Rachel's aunts, uncles, cousins and friends, both in this country and around the globe. All are affected in their own way.

Rachel's niece and nephews will now never know their aunt and, for my part, it is going to be very hard seeing our granddaughter Belinda reaching the age of 21, then 22 and 23, always wondering what Rachel would be like by this age.

Her friends will never get over her loss, especially Saoirse with whom she had spent her childhood and youth. This girl was so traumatised she had to leave Hull after Rachel's funeral as she could no longer face living in the town. There are so many more of them like her.

There's Adam, an old school friend, who asked that his own crucifix be placed in Rachel's coffin. And what of Patrick, our neighbour's son, who also loved Rachel from afar? He didn't wash or shave the entire time she was missing and was so distraught he could not even attend her funeral. He could only send his apologies instead.

The most important, the most crucial player in this pitiful scenario, is Rachel herself. Our grief is nothing compared to the fact that her life has been taken, and so cruelly. All of her potential has been stolen and she has been robbed of the chance of motherhood, which she really craved. Her life obliterated, her brilliant light snuffed out as if it were nothing, by a vile creature who thought not at all of consequences on that fateful night.

April 2003

I'm alone in the house today when the telephone rings. It is Paul Davison, the lead detective. He needs to meet with us this week, though will not say for what reason and I don't press the issue. It could be just another minor detail to do with the case but, somehow, I don't think so, especially as the request is for us to attend police HQ, as opposed to him dropping into our place.

Ray will need to take time off work, which won't be a problem, but something is telling me that he ought not to accompany me to this interview. Instead, it is agreed by 'the boss' and I that I will attend with my daughter, Vanda. I will mention the telephone call to Ray, but play it down so as not to alarm him. After all, what cause can there be for alarm? We have merely been asked to go along and speak to the police; this ominous feeling I have is probably only my overactive imagination playing havoc.

Vanda, though, is as unnerved by this unexpected invitation (to discuss what?) as I myself am and is equally worried by it. We both have a feeling that it is something we will not want to hear. That whatever it is will not be good and we are also in strong agreement that it could affect Ray badly. I can't imagine what makes us assume that, or what makes us think that we will be better able to handle any given situation than will Ray, but the decision is made and we'll stick to it. Let's hope we are both over-reacting.

Two days later, we are at police HQ in the early afternoon as arranged and are taken to the Operations room, where Paul Davison has his office. It's barely big enough to accommodate the three of us and I see on the desk, which dominates the room, a file with Rachel's name written on the front. I can't help but notice that it is dreadfully dog-eared.

The boss, unusually for him, appears rather ill at ease and I feel very apprehensive, although I don't know why. What can he possibly have to tell us that is any worse than has already happened?

After exchanging a few pleasantries, no doubt with a view to putting us at our ease, he gets straight to the point. As he begins, I see that he is looking at us both intently. Maybe he is worried as to what our reactions will be when he drops his bombshell. And a massive bombshell it is, for the pair of us.

He tells us that forensic evidence has come back and shows that sexual intercourse had taken place around the time of Rachel's death. Furthermore, DNA tests prove, beyond a shadow of a doubt, that Michael Little was the person responsible for that act. It cannot be ascertained whether or not this happened before or after her death, or 'pre- or post-mortem', as the police put it, but they are of the opinion that it was post-mortem. That aspect may sink in later but, for now, to learn that it happened at all is a monumental blow.

It had been our greatest concern when Rachel's body was found, three months ago, that she had not been violated sexually. It was Vanda who had asked the question and was told unequivocally that, no, nothing like that had occurred. And when she asked how they were so sure, the reply was that Rachel was fully clothed when found. There has been no further mention of the subject until now.

I don't particularly feel any surprise despite that. I am just speechless and utterly bereft that, on top of all else, my daughter had suffered that indignity. We are assured that: '... sometimes evidence can take a lot of time to sift through before any conclusions can be reached'. And with that, we have to be satisfied.

My question to Paul Davison is this: how does he think Michael Little will react? The reply is that, even as we three are speaking, Little is at another police station being interviewed. He had been brought back to Hull during the morning for that very purpose. It will not come as a shock to him, however, because his solicitor had already been informed of this new evidence. He'd told his client what he was about to be confronted with. Little probably knew before we did.

Vanda and I are totally devastated but I think we conducted ourselves well, considering this calamitous news. I know now that it was in Ray's, and probably everyone else's, best interests that he is not in this office here today. This news will destroy him completely and I don't know how I am going to break it to him when he gets home. The thought fills me with dread and I can't begin to guess at what his reaction will be.

After Ray drops Vanda home following our meeting with Paul Davison, he is very quiet and seems distracted. I assume that Vanda has disclosed the day's grim findings concerning Rachel. I say nothing, thinking it best to allow him his own thoughts on the subject. I am, in any case, finding it hard to come to terms with the revelations myself, despondent and definitely not in the mood for confrontations of any kind.

Today, on speaking to Vanda, I discover that she had said nothing to Ray and imagined that I had done so by now, a dilemma if ever there was! The onus is certainly on me now to be the bearer of this terrible news and I can't wait much longer.

It's even worse than I imagined when I finally pluck up the courage to broach the subject with Ray and so very difficult to find the right words. When I manage to get the point across to him, he goes wild and is on the telephone to Paul Davison almost before I finish speaking. I don't want to hear the words – it is enough to know that he is totally beyond reason, such is his anger, shock, sadness and the length of time it has taken for us to find out what really happened.

Ray demands that Paul Davison charge Michael Little with rape in addition to abduction and murder. I don't know the response to this but find out later that the police simply do not have the evidence to prove rape. I am just mortified at the way my husband is laying into the Chief of Police who, to be fair, has a job to do and that job has its limitations.

I can understand Ray's wrath as, hopefully, Paul Davison will. I am sure this is not the first time he has been verbally abused by someone who is overwrought past the point of no return. We all react differently. All I can say is that *my* reaction was the direct opposite of Ray's when I learned of the sexual aspect of the case. Suffice to say, we are both shattered at this turn of events and it is yet another thing that we will have to contend with in the months leading up to the trial.

In a couple of weeks, Michael Little is due to appear in court for his plea and directions hearing. I wonder what, if anything, is going on in his vapid mind in the meantime?

Friday, 23 May 2003

When the judge announces that Michael Little will stand trial at Hull Crown Court on 13 October 2003 it comes as a surprise to everyone. Little has pleaded not guilty to Rachel's murder but we had fully expected the trial to be held in another city – Sheffield or Leeds perhaps.

There have been several delays in the run-up to the plea and directions hearing. The first of these hearings – on 2 May – had turned into a fiasco, with arguments ranging from Little wanting to change his solicitor to 'submissions of not fit to plead', due to 'diminished responsibility'. To our relief, it has all been to no avail, and on 23 May we learn he will be pleading not guilty. We have been warned that this would be the most likely path he would take, and even what his defence is sure to be.

Even so, it is still a massive blow to us when his brief announces that he will be alleging that Rachel had in fact gone up to his flat voluntarily, that consensual sex had taken place, and that he, Little, did not kill her. A third person had done that but would not be named in the court that day.

Words cannot begin to describe how it feels to hear such a dreadful statement read out, to hear the actual words. Or to see Little stand there seemingly without a care in the world, knowing that we, her family and poor Mark, who loved her so desperately, have to listen to these blatant lies. Because this beast does not have the guts to admit what he did to Rachel that night, her name will now be dragged through the mud in his attempt to make himself the victim.

Mark is inconsolable while we, the rest of her family, are furiously angry. We are very frustrated but, more than anything, intensely sad that the character of our beloved girl is to be torn to shreds in a court of law, in order that her killer receive 'justice'.

Devastation and depression really set in the minute we leave the courtroom but we are assured by the police and the prosecution lawyers that we need have no worries. Everything is proceeding as they expect it to and the case for Little does not stand up to scrutiny. They are all very confident of a conviction since the evidence against him is overwhelming. We must put our faith in our team now as there is nothing else we can do.

Our feelings towards Michael Little were already murderous but, knowing a bit more about him now, they are compounded. He is a hefty individual, seeming more so with each successive appearance since January. Standing 5ft 9in and weighing around 16 stone, he has dark hair and is bearded with pale skin and eyes. I would describe his expression as inscrutable and his appearance as scruffy, even in court.

We know that he is the product of a broken home, with one older full brother and four younger half-sisters. He has had a chequered upbringing and was a problem child, out of control by the time he was 13. Social Services were called in at that point but he had already earned a reputation as a bully and a petty thief.

He was excluded from school on more than one occasion, and his attendance record was just 22 per cent. He left for good, with no qualifications, at 16. Since then he has failed to hold down a job for any length of time due to his bad attitude, tardiness and inertia. He has few friends and has never been known to have had a girlfriend, but he is a fantasist. He is known to have told his few friends that he was seeing a '6ft blonde supermodel'. It was all in his mind and this figment of his imagination was certainly not Rachel.

In his later teens, Little became known to the police. There was, perhaps, nothing to suggest that he would turn into a killer, but worrying signs, nonetheless.

Before moving into a flat near Rachel and Mark, he had lived alone at two previous addresses in the east of the city. He was evicted from the second for non-payment of rent and returned to the family home. Within a very short space of time, however, he was given the tenancy of another council property.

We are told that he lived in squalor and that he is a filthy and unkempt individual. Most days he does not arise until the afternoon, having spent the whole night listening to music, watching videos and smoking cannabis. He has been known to experiment with amphetamines, and is a drinker.

When questioned about his employment record, he purports to be unable to work, citing numerous ailments ranging from headaches to depression and ulcerated legs. Rachel would not have given him a second glance and he, in turn, was not fit to lick her boots.

Having seen him now on two occasions, I am also more and more convinced this is the man who walked past our house on the morning of 1 January.

All we can do now is wait until the trial begins on 13 October. Perhaps we will then get the answers we have been seeking over the last five months. It is out of our hands now but it is going to be a very long and difficult wait for us.

June 2003

Half a year has now gone by since Rachel walked into the night, never to return. Those six months seem to have flown past without us noticing but now we are marking time until October. It will be here before we know it.

It is hard to recall that, when this nightmare began, it was darkest winter. We have seen spring come and go and now summer is upon us. The glorious weather is meaningless, since one day is much the same as another, one week no different to the last. There is no pleasure in anything at all for me nor, I suspect, for any of us.

During the early part of this month, we hold a memorial service for Rachel. We had decided we wanted to do this after a contingent of her neighbours arrived at our house, bearing a book of condolence and some money they had collected locally. Their wish was that we use this donation to erect some form of plaque in Rachel's memory. We thought this a lovely gesture on their part.

Having considered all options, we came to the conclusion that any sort of plaque would be at risk of vandalism if it was in a public place, sad though that sounds. Thus we came up with the idea of asking Rachel's local priest, Father Wood, if we could put it in the foyer of his church and, at the same time, allow us to hold some sort of memorial service there. He was happy to do this and also agreed that a fellow priest and friend of ours, Father Pat Day, could lead the service for us. We then called upon John Murray, a good friend who is an excellent musician, to direct the whole affair.

After the traumatic events of May – the plea and directions hearing and all that entailed – planning the memorial is a form of respite for us. To begin with, I am as keen as Ray for this service to take place but, as the day draws nearer, I am becoming more and more apprehensive about the whole thing. There is a great deal of organisation involved and each of us has our own ideas about what Rachel would have liked. This causes some friction at times, but, if the truth be known, none of us apart from Mark really knew her tastes in music and verse. He is getting somewhat uptight about it all, feels it is too soon after her funeral for a memorial service, and that he is being pushed out of the arrangements. I can understand his feelings as I am starting to feel the same way myself.

Ray is becoming obsessed with it, spending hours worrying about how it will come across, poring over books and articles (religious and other) so that it will be just right on the night. He has said from the start that he intends to speak during the service and, although I am a little taken aback by this, I decide not to interfere. It will be enough for me to organise the buffet, which we will have afterwards in the club adjoining the church. Vanda has managed to get a group of Rachel and Mark's friends to do the entertainment for this. We are expecting a good turn-out and the event is well publicised.

Ray is spending a lot of time working on the eulogy for Rachel and getting into quite a state about it. We eventually decide on the hymns and readings, though not easily, with a lot of help from our musical director. Above all, it should be light-hearted and not at all like the funeral. It is meant to be a happy occasion but for me it is becoming fraught with doubt and trepidation because Ray is so het up over it. I am losing interest now and feel surplus to requirements. This is his show and so let him get on with it. With his help, I cater for around 150 people and that's enough to keep my mind off other things. Everything is falling into place and we need only to deliver the food etc. to the club and present ourselves at the church for the service.

I don't know what Ray's eulogy contains but ask only one thing of him: whatever he intends to say, we – her family – are included in his musings and it is not just his own personal memories of Rachel. He colours up slightly and replies, 'Of course not.' I begin to wonder, but do not press the issue.

The church is almost full, although the very people for whom we initially thought up this service – the neighbours who made the collection – do not appear. Nor, to my disappointment, do any of Rachel's school friends, most of whom will have known about it. The press and television are in attendance, together with a small police presence.

I find it all very, very stressful and wish I were anywhere other than in this place right now. That is not to say it doesn't go down well, as Father Pat and John Murray are both so experienced in such matters that they do us proud. The readers, including Father White, our own priest and friend, are all we could hope for. The only heart-stopping moment comes when Vanda, on leaving the altar, misses her footing and almost falls the rest of the way. In my nervous and apprehensive state, I want to burst into hysterical laughter, but Vanda is very shaken by this incident.

The television cameras are very near us and I am embarrassed by this. I feel that they are watching me in the hope that I might break down but I am too keyed up for that to happen, nor would I shed my tears in public.

Now comes the time for Ray to approach the lectern to deliver his eulogy. I know he is extremely nervous, so I give his arm a squeeze of encouragement and wonder what is about to be said. To say I am shocked is an understatement and, should Ray read this, he may be surprised to know it. Did I make a mistake in thinking he would be the voice for all of us, that he would speak of the love we all had for Rachel and how hard it will be for us to go through life without her?

His words, though beautiful and eloquent, speak only of his own love for her, of his own memories and his own sorrow. I find that I can't even look at him while he is speaking, and each word is like a body blow as he continues. Am I being selfish and unreasonable in thinking that this eulogy would include all of us or is that what a eulogy is, a very personal thing?

My heart turns over when Ray says that he was 'mad about Rachel' and I realise, not for the first time, the depth of his feeling for her. In my distressed state, I feel that nothing else now is of any importance to him – not I, nor any of our other three children. That my own love for Rachel, my own sorrow at her loss, is as nothing compared to his. I don't know how I'll get through the ordeal of the buffet and entertainment.

Another disappointment awaits in the club afterwards, when not many people adjourn there after the service. The music, though excellent, is far too loud in a half-empty hall, so any conversation is impossible. The entertainers, including Mark, are in good voice and enjoy themselves, but for me the poignancy is almost too much to bear. Rachel should be part of this, she should be here amongst us, but, if she were, it would not be taking place anyway. It is very hard to keep smiling.

I feel shattered when we reach home and very withdrawn from everything. Ray, I am sure, has noticed my demeanour, and may even suspect why I am so quiet but we have little to say to each other. Feeling so drained and exhausted is good enough reason to skirt around issues which should be tackled, is my own thought, even though I know it would be far better to bring things out into the open, to sit down together and speak rationally of our individual feelings. I sense that Ray is deeply disappointed in my failure to congratulate him on his eulogy, which most people have deemed marvellous. If I were to begin to discuss it with him, I would be afraid of saying the wrong thing, of upsetting him or hurting his feelings, of kicking him when he is down. The whole situation is so very, very sad and he himself so destroyed that I could never add to that. Nor do I want to run the risk of confrontation, which could so easily happen.

This has been such a traumatic happening. It is beyond anyone's imagination and it is not something that one is taught how to handle, so we don't know how. Inconsequential things, like not being included in Ray's eulogy, are becoming like personal slurs to me, along with other inane occurrences which would be laughable under other circumstances.

I am feeling more and more misunderstood; maybe that is my own fault. I keep my feelings so well hidden that few people know them, whereas Ray is open with his. His grief is there for all to see, while mine is not, but it is no different. I feel that I am punishing myself by keeping quiet, even harming myself both physically and mentally, and wonder if this is normal behaviour. Do all those who suffer a loss such as this feel the same despair, the same anger and resentment? Do they too want to hit out at their nearest and dearest in order to assuage their own sorrow? I only know that I am beyond consolation and, at the moment, feel like I am walking a tightrope.

I get up each morning and go through the motions, yet it feels like I am watching a film in which I play no part. How can life go on all around me as if everything is normal, when the world has gone mad? How can it act as if things are the same as they were on 31 December, when they will never ever be the same again? Each day it becomes harder – harder to pretend I am coping, when my every thought is of Rachel, only of Rachel. Terrible images tear me apart, both day and night. Trying always to conjure up her face in my mind and failing to do so. The horror of what happened to my defenceless, youngest child, how she must have suffered, and the overwhelming desire for answers. Not the precise details of how she died, but the need to know the circumstances surrounding her death – how that monster was able to overpower her and get her up into his hovel. It is all-consuming. My mind will never rest until I know that much, at least.

I can see this family becoming more fragmented with every passing day, yet I feel there is nothing I can do about it. Despite my outward demeanour of calmness, I am totally destroyed inside. It is as if something is squeezing the very life out of my body and I am unable to fight against it. If I were to do so, I fear that I would lose control completely and I cannot let that happen. I must keep going, at least until the trial, for Rachel's sake, until her name is cleared and she is exonerated of all blame. She must be seen, by everyone, as the innocent girl she was in all this. The world must know it and I owe it to her that the truth be told. So I must try to keep my head, stay calm and, above all, not dwell on the forthcoming trial.

I have been informed that I am to be called as the only family witness but that does not worry me. I am not afraid for myself, nor of facing once more the evil creature who snuffed out Rachel's life so cruelly. I am not afraid of standing up to the barrister who is defending him, but I am very much afraid of letting Rachel down. Of saying the wrong thing and of having to listen to the pack of blatant lies Little will undoubtedly resort to in order to blacken my daughter's character so she becomes the one to blame and her cowardly murderer the victim.

I feel very much alone now and unable to voice my innermost thoughts and fears, even to my husband of 40 years. It is as if a wedge has been driven between the two of us, and our only son, who remains at home with us, is caught in the middle of it all. We three are living together – yet apart – in the same house. We seem to have separate lives at the moment, each of us inhabiting different rooms and rarely coming together.

We all dwell on Rachel's fate but none of us wants to voice

those thoughts aloud. Certainly we don't discuss our doubts and fears. It is too painful. Each of us has our own theory about what happened and they don't always tie in with the other's, so there have been some heated moments and probably more to come. Therefore, it is better that we say nothing, rather than say things that we will regret in the future.

To those outside our little circle, this must seem strange behaviour. One would likely imagine that we would draw closer together and take strength from each other but this is just not happening. I know that Kerry finds this very hard to understand but she does not live among us, nor has she experienced the atmosphere that prevails from day to day in our once happy home. In the absence of family and close friends near by, we have only each other now, and it seems familiarity is beginning to breed contempt. The police visits dried up long ago, apart from the odd times when they need to impart some snippet of news to us. We, Rachel's family, are no better informed than the general public as to what exactly befell her on that night, though we do know the cause of her death.

Naturally, we have our own theories, but we have been told nothing concrete concerning the case. It is understandable that we cannot be given inside information at random, nor would we want the responsibility of knowing everything that the police know. Indeed, it is vital to us that nothing is said beforehand that might jeopardise the trial, so we must wait until October to hear the facts.

Even so, the frustration is unbearable – wanting to know and yet not wanting to know the ordeal that Rachel had to suffer. Imagining every scenario and going over, again and again, the whys, the wherefores, the ifs, the butsÖ Driving ourselves mad, dealing with the bits of definite information we have been given. It just does not bear thinking about. I can get to the point where Rachel was accosted, however that may have happened, but when I think of the terror that must have ensued, my mind shuts down. After all this time, I have yet to break down and grieve for Rachel's loss and I never cease to wonder how this can be.

She was my youngest child and I dearly loved and cherished her. Her loss is indescribable, so why am I unable to shed bitter tears, knowing that she is never going to come back again? In the deep of the night, when sleep eludes me, I try to analyse my bizarre behaviour and the only answer I can come up with is that I am still in deep shock – I am not yet ready to accept that this terrible thing has happened. Not to Rachel, and not to us, an ordinary family living everyday lives. It does not seem possible that a stranger could kill my child, almost on her own doorstep, in an area where I grew up. This is the stuff of Stephen King books and horror movies – not the kind of thing that happens to people like us. I still haven't faced up to the fact that it *has* happened, and it worries me greatly that I never will.

Early July 2003

I haven't gone back to work yet, though both John and Ray have done. Work, and the fact that at some point I shall have to return, does not enter my thoughts at all. I am grateful that no pressure has been put upon me so far to go back and my salary continues to be paid each month. Ray felt he ought to resume work some weeks ago – not because he missed going out each day but because he knew his company would not indulge him indefinitely. For my part, I couldn't care less right now.

Vanda's health continues to decline due to her diabetes and failing kidneys and I spend part of most days helping her out if needed, although it is mostly transport to her various hospital appointments and to the shops that she requires. This is yet another heartache. Were I able to donate a kidney to her, I would do so tomorrow. Unfortunately, I know I am not a match and so we must hope that one becomes available before

...is to spend too long on dialysis, which is looking imminent. Of all the family, she alone seems to have some understanding of how I am feeling, perhaps because we have similar temperaments.

A few weeks earlier, I lost interest in doing anything at all. I had no energy or even the inclination, to cook, clean or shop. All the things I normally enjoy have palled for me and I can find no pleasure in anything. After a short time, however, my better self took control and I am now cooking and baking again to a certain extent. As well as this, I have done some rearranging of the rooms, bought a few new pieces of furniture and have found some solace in the garden. I have a dedicated plot solely for Rachel, and there are various plants and shrubs named especially for her. It comforts me somewhat to be among nature and to imagine that she is out there with me.

The daily visits to the cemetery continue as they have from the day we laid her to rest. I get no consolation at all in being there but I do not want her grave to look unkempt or uncared for. Choosing a headstone does not figure highly at the moment. It is enough to know that the flowers are renewed regularly and are looking as nice as I can make them.

Ray visits her at least twice a day, though he too has said that he draws no comfort from this. Initially, we would go together, but that doesn't happen much nowadays for several reasons. For my part, it just became too stressful for me to observe Ray's utter distress each time he approached the grave. To see his tears, to watch how his face crumpled up and the accompanying tuneless humming he would emit was just too heartbreaking for me to cope with. I can offer him no comfort, because I have none to give. I think we are becoming a little selfish and – dare I say it – a little angry with each other. I now feel that he doesn't want me there with him and he can grieve more freely when he is on his own.

Quite often, too, there are members of the public by Rachel's grave and this upsets and annoys me somewhat at times. I do not know them and they do not know me but some of them have a morbid curiosity about her death. I cannot, nor do I want to, discuss this with anyone and I see these people as intruding on my privacy and my grief. Ray, on the other hand, has a totally different attitude to it. He is glad to talk to strangers about Rachel and considers that she has become public property, so he feels it is only right that he converse with them. In the beginning, doing fresh floral displays for her each day helped to keep me sane but it is starting to wear off a little now. Lately I feel I am just going through the motions.

I haven't exactly become reclusive, but I do not welcome visitors unless they are acceptable to me. Since we are not especially sociable people, this is not entirely unusual. I am putting off in particular a promised visit from some of my work colleagues. I know that they have good intentions but what could we possibly talk about, I wonder? The forthcoming court case is definitely taboo for obvious reasons and I am just unable to indulge in small talk at the moment. I certainly don't wish to hear about work, nor about their daughters when mine is dead.

For the same reason, I will drive miles out of my way to go shopping, partly so I don't bump into anyone I may be acquainted with but mainly so that I am on unfamiliar ground. Rachel and I went many places together but I cannot face any of them alone. Everywhere I go I think I see her and many times I have had to stop myself from buying her a book, or some item she would have liked. It is so very, very hard to imagine that she is never going to be with me again on my travels. I find it particularly poignant to see girls of Rachel's age pushing prams and buggies and knowing that she will never be a mother. Unless our son eventually settles down, there will be no more grandchildren for us. I will never take out my needles and hooks to make a layette for Rachel's babies, as I would have done. It seems so very unfair that this unspeakable thing should happen to *her*, when there are so many bad people in this world.

I never cease to be horrified when I see and hear youngsters out on the streets at all hours and think of the dangers that could befall them. In the main, they have probably never known anything different, whereas Rachel had been cosseted and protected from day one. Despite this, she still came to grief. The odds of that happening must be considerably greater than winning the lottery. How ironic can that be and how hard for parents like us to accept, who were always so very conscientious?

The stifling days continue and I am keeping myself busy. Ray is withdrawing further into himself and I know that I am no help or comfort to him. There are so many things that could and should be said but the days go by and nothing is said. It is slightly less fraught on the rare occasions when we have visitors, so obviously we do need to talk, just not to each other it seems. The long silences are terrible and any conversation we do have is stilted. I can do nothing about it as I feel too shattered and so very angry. It seems like not one person can understand how I am feeling and no doubt Ray feels the same way about his own emotions.

To me, it seems that each of us – especially we, her parents – feels that we alone have lost Rachel. That we alone are the one who feels her loss the most and are suffering the most. That she was more important to us than to any other family member or to Mark, her boyfriend. I myself feel that I, as her mother, must surely have figured higher in her life than anybody else, yet I am sure that Ray feels that, as her father, he was her priority. Common sense, along with my knowledge of Rachel, tells me that none of this is true. She thought no more or less of either of us and cared for each of her siblings equally. None of us can know how she truly felt about Mark, who knew her in a completely different way to any of us. The pain and hurt that poor boy is suffering goes beyond any words and each successive day is taking its toll on him. God only knows how he is going to cope with the trial when it comes. I would give anything to spare him that ordeal.

Mid-July 2003

Recently we have had a visit from the police. There is always some ulterior motive for their seemingly out-of-the-blue calls and this one was no exception. It seems that the potential witness Michael Little named is unwilling to co-operate with the police. They say that he may have to be subpoenaed as a hostile witness and this is a little worrying. They tell us some of the content of the defence statement and, were it not so tragic, it would be laughable. We are assured again that there is no plausible defence and we have no reason to worry about the outcome, but of course we do.

The fact that Little may change his plea to guilty at the start of the trial is again mooted and we have mixed feelings about this. On the one hand, we would love to spare Mark's – and our own – feelings but would the public ever know the true story were this to happen? Many rumours abound on the estate where her murder occurred and I want to silence, once and for all, those gossipmongers and doubters. That may only be possible if the not guilty plea stands and the trial runs its course. When the time comes, I know that there will be shocks for everyone and terrible things will be told. I don't know how I will endure hearing the stark reality of it, or how I will take that stand without cracking up, should the finger be pointed at Rachel.

At times I torment myself so much about what happened to her, trying to put pieces of the puzzle together and coming up empty-handed, that I think I am going insane. These are the times when I want to confront the police and ask them to tell me exactly what they know. Of course, this is not possible and I don't suppose it would make me feel any better, knowing now, rather than when the time comes. It is futile trying to discuss these thoughts with Ray because he has said that he never wants to know what happened to Rachel. The fact that she is gone from him is his sole concern; anything else is just too much for him to handle. I, on the other hand, feel I can never put this behind me and get on with my life until I face up to everything that happened that night. The need to know is like a cancer eating into me.

One of the things that the police have been able to confirm is that the man who walked past Rachel and me on the morning of New Year's Day was indeed Michael Little. Knowing this makes my blood run cold. To think that this is the person whom I considered asking to walk Rachel home for her safety does not bear contemplation. It is of no help to me whatsoever when Kerry says that, had I done so, the outcome would have been very different. How, I wonder, does she think that makes me feel? It may well have ended differently, but, at the same time, the outcome could and, I believe, would have been the same. How much worse, then, would I feel, knowing that I, her mother, had sent her off happily with her murderer?

I am angry, furiously angry at many things, but especially that the onus seems to be on me in all of this. I was the last person with Rachel before she left our home that morning. I and I alone could have saved her and I did not. I shall have to live with that for the rest of my life. Hindsight is a wonderful thing.

Late July/August 2003

The summer drags on interminably and one day runs into another. I am trying to keep busy but I feel totally exhausted from the moment I get up each morning. Sleep eludes me and I often wonder how I manage to get by with so little of it, but somehow I do. The night hours are horrendous when I awake suddenly with Rachel on my mind. I haven't really dreamed about her, nor had nightmares – she's just there with me all the time. Lately when I wake up during the night, my thoughts go immediately to her drawing close to her home and this vile creature waiting there for her, as we know he must have been. When I let myself think about what must have happened then, a feeling of great terror assails me. My heart beats so fast that I think it must surely stop altogether. Often I feel my face start to twitch and think I am having a stroke, but would it really matter?

Why, oh why didn't I walk home with her as I had

considered doing at the time? Why should Rachel, a defenceless girl, have been caught on her own? The unfairness and horror of it all is just too much to bear. I wish, how I wish, I had gone with her, then perhaps it would have been me instead of her that he killed. I feel that my death rather than Rachel's would be so much easier for everybody to get over.

I know that I am becoming more irrational, more paranoid, with every passing day. I am starting to imagine that nobody is on my side, and that the only time I was of any use was in the early days of Rachel's disappearance. I served my purpose then, but, now that period is over, my usefulness is past – or so it seems to me in my present state of mind. I feel totally and utterly worthless, completely without support and understanding, and an object of contempt.

Is this, then, the price I have to pay for being seen as the strong one in all this, the one who appears to be in control of her feelings? If only people knew how out of control my feelings really are beneath this false exterior I show. But I cannot tell them and they cannot guess, so I am my own worst enemy. I have never been able to show my feelings and this is seen by some as misplaced pride. I am not proud, nor am I cold, but I will admit that I am very reserved and have a need to keep my dignity at all times. This is me: it has always been my nature, just as it is Ray's nature to shout and rage and to let his feelings be known unconditionally.

It does not make any difference in the end. We are both still suffering and neither one of us is feeling this any more or less than the other. The only difference is that I was the one who carried Rachel for nine months, the one who gave birth to her and the one who nurtured her at the start of her life. A mother's role is unique and quite different to that of a father, sister or brother. In the main, they do not change the dirty nappies, endure the sleepless nights, nor nurse a child through its ills. When a mother loses her child, it is as if a part of her own body has been torn away and that is how I feel now. I would feel exactly the same way were it any one of my children. Fathers play their part, but it is the mother who bears the brunt of any child's upbringing. At least, any mother who is worthy of the name does so.

How then, can a mother come to terms with the loss of that child? To lose a child to an illness, or even an accident, is one thing but to lose a child in the way that Rachel was lost goes beyond all reason and I think I am rapidly losing mine. Only the mother of a murdered son or daughter could possibly understand this. I say this without any disrespect to Ray's feelings.

The month of August continues but it hasn't had a hope from the start. On the 1st it was our 40th wedding anniversary and one we might have celebrated under normal circumstances. Obviously, there is no reason to do so this year and we both agree the night before that we won't be making anything of the day. Why then am I so cut up and hurt not to receive a card from Ray? My self-esteem is at an all-time low and I imagine that I mean nothing to him now, after all we have been through over the years. The fact that he has lost Rachel overrides all else in his life now, or so it seems to me.

We have not seen or heard from Mark in some time now, although Ray has tried to contact him on several occasions, as has Vanda. He knows he is welcome to visit us whenever he wants but he is reticent at the best of times. Perhaps he has his own reasons for not getting in touch or maybe, as I suspect, he is just withdrawing further into himself. As far as I am aware, he has not been called as a witness at the trial of Michael Little and I hope it remains that way. I have my doubts as to whether he could face up to the vicious cross-examination of the defence, whereas I think I have the strength to do so.

Kerry is awarded a BA Honours degree in Fine Art and it is a small glimmer of light in the gloom. Her father and I drive down to Southampton to view an exhibition she has put on for the end of her course. I had no idea beforehand that she has dedicated her work entirely to Rachel and it upsets me to find out, beautiful though it was. She has done a lot of work with photographs of Rachel and several now adorn our house. A portrait is also in the process of being painted. Once this is completed and in place, it will be another nail in my coffin, another constant reminder that Rachel is no longer with us. Only her pictures remain.

A couple of weeks later Kerry comes up to our part of the world with her husband and their eldest boy. She is considering moving back to be nearer to us, but I believe it is only a pipe dream and nothing will come of it. It is a respite for me to have her here even for a few days and the atmosphere is somewhat lightened. I know she is losing patience with me, unable to understand how I feel. How could she know when I can't understand myself, my mind is such a turmoil of emotions. I fear that I am cutting myself off from my children and so they, in turn, are gravitating towards their father. Do I come across as so cold-hearted and therefore not in need of consideration? Do they imagine that because I appear to be getting on with my life I am not shattered beyond belief? Every day is torture, every day sees me sinking further and further into despair and I think I am becoming severely depressed. Surely this is all a nightmare from which I shall awaken to find Rachel bounding in the door?

It is especially hard for me when Belinda, our granddaughter, flies over to Ireland for her first holiday there. It brings back so many memories of the time Rachel spent a month there alone with her cousins. Ray's family ask us constantly to go over there and visit but I think they are beginning to realise their pleas are falling on deaf ears. There is no way that I could face all the old familiar places and people, no way I could face all their well-meant sympathies. Nor could I face seeing the cousins, who are all of a similar age and appearance to Rachel. Not now and maybe not ever will I be able to face it all. It is just too poignant.

Mid-August 2003

During Rachel's disappearance and after she was found, we received, among other messages, one from her ex-colleagues at the creche. They were keen to dedicate part of a garden to her, which is situated not far away. A plaque was erected and various shrubs planted in her memory. The thought behind it was sincere but seeing Rachel's name, and the dates of her birth and death, filled me with horror. The same applied with the plaque we put up in the church at the time of her memorial service. After the initial dedication at the Rainbow Garden, I have been back there only once, to plant a few more plants and shrubs.

Ray, however, visits the gardens regularly, though I don't know whether he draws comfort from it. I imagine he doesn't want it to grow into disarray but I just don't feel able to go there myself. I hope he doesn't look on my reluctance to visit as yet another sign of my petulance. I simply just can't bear to see these tangible signs of her death because they force me to admit that she is gone forever and I don't want to do that. I don't think I am in denial because I *do* realise she isn't coming back. I am just not ready, nor do I want, to let her go yet and unless I see actual proof, like the plaques, I can pretend that she is still here. I can pretend that she is living in another part of the country, like Kerry does, and she just hasn't been in touch for a while. It is the only way I can cope for the moment, although that may change.

It would be lovely to have some sign that she is indeed somewhere on a higher plane and we will meet up with her again someday. Sadly, I cannot believe that is so. If she were around, I know that she would have given me some sign but there has been nothing. I have not lost my faith in God but I cannot begin to imagine why He would let this happen to someone like Rachel. I am becoming more angry with every passing day that the perpetrator of this crime is still alive while she is dead. That he dared to lay a hand on her, to strike her, to knife her to death. That he then hid her broken body in a dirty coal shed, where it lay in an undignified state for a whole month before detection. It beggars belief.

Were he to be incarcerated for the rest of his days, that would not be justice and I defy anyone to say otherwise. Let those who scream for rehabilitation walk in our shoes for just one day. Let them endure the terror that Rachel must have felt as he stabbed her almost 30 times and perhaps then they can speak of forgiveness. I have none – no forgiveness and no pity. I wish only harm to Michael Little and to anyone whom he holds dear. I could kill him with my bare hands, even though it would not bring Rachel back. It would, however, avenge her and that is no more than she deserves and would have expected from us. Because that kind of justice is never going to take place, my fervent desire is that, whatever sentence Little is given, he serves every day of it in living fear of his life. When the prison fraternity learn the true facts of what he did to her, I want him to be as terrified as she was. It would make me very happy to know that he was thrashed on a regular basis, and if I am damned for saying this, so be it. Let those who disagree keep quiet until it happens to them.

Now the evenings are growing shorter and the trial is less than two months away. The summer is drawing to a close and I know the time is going to fly by from now onwards. We know Ray's brother will be here for the trial, and Kerry too, and that is heartening for me. We will need all the support we can get when the time comes. It is my intention to be there every day, although I know it will be traumatic. I can't let Rachel down but I am unsure of Ray's intentions at this stage – it may all be too much for him.

At the moment, I can see no further than the trial, but wonder if it will all be a big anti-climax. After it is all over, it will be make-or-break time for us. We either try to get our lives back again or we sink further into despondency. Who can say what will happen? I am going to make a concerted effort to regain some sort of normalcy for the sake of our other three children but it will be very hard. I believe that we, their parents, owe it to them to show that they, too, are everything to us. I don't want to ever lose sight of that fact and I hope the three of them realise that too.

Ray is becoming more and more interested in visiting a medium after Kerry and our niece Liesel did so, Kerry in Southampton and Liesel in Ireland. Both felt that they received positive messages and drew comfort from this. These messages seemed plausible to me too but I feel no desire to become involved in such mysteries. I am more than a little surprised that Ray is so taken with the idea, as the Ray of old would have been very sceptical. However, this is not the Ray I once knew. He has changed completely from the macho man I once thought he was to a totally different version of himself. I have now become the strong one, or perhaps I always was beneath my acquiescent exterior. I know now he will not rest until he visits a medium in the desperate hope that Rachel will be there with a message for him. If that happens, he might gain some comfort from it but, equally, it could make him question even more.

I don't dismiss out of hand what was said to Kerry or to Liesel, but I don't need to go myself because I feel that Rachel is with me at all times, that her spirit is around me wherever I go and that is enough for me at the moment. Her earthly being is gone from me forever but she will stay alive in my heart. This is how I, personally, think that those we have loved and lost live on. Should Rachel ever send me a sign to the contrary, I will be waiting here until the time when my life, too, is ended, and who knows? Perhaps then I will see her once more.

Saturday, 16 August 2003

Ray and Vanda are going to a town some 20 miles away where a medium is to appear in a theatre. Ray had said previously that he would never go to see anyone in our own town, since our faces are well known now. There would be a risk of being recognised and so any of us would be an easy target.

On this day, I am feeling very unwell with a headache that will not go away and does not respond to medication. This apart, I have no wish to go with them, not even for the ride out. I only hope Ray is not too upset at the outcome of the evening. If there are no messages, he may well be, but, if there are, he could make himself even worse. I worry about him driving home in a distressed state. During this week, he has already crashed the boat he works on, as well as his car. Thankfully, nobody came to grief on either occasion but increasingly he seems to be in a world of his own, unable to take anything in. I feel that I am to blame in some way because

I am not giving him enough support or compassion. It is so very hard.

I don't know what time to expect Ray home but certainly not before 11pm. I feel no better following my bath and go to bed in the hope of my head clearing. This night I am up and down almost every hour (as I am most nights), and finally decide to come downstairs at 3.30am. My head still pounds and I don't return to bed until 6.30am, which means I don't arise properly until almost 10am.

During the day, nothing is mentioned about the visit to the medium, so I don't know if the trip was a success, though I guess not. We seem to have sunk further into despondency and are unable to communicate at all today. I feel no better physically, despite having dosed myself with copious amounts of painkillers, and at 4pm, for the first time in my life, I go and lie down, and don't get up again until late in the evening.

I don't noticeably improve over the next few days and wonder if I might have picked up some sort of virus. Perhaps it could be depression manifesting itself. Eventually all things catch up with a person and there is surely a limit to how long one can keep up a front?

Vanda isn't too well at the moment so I must rouse myself and go round there. She tells me that the visit to the medium was rubbish and she felt only embarrassment throughout the entire show. She thought the medium was a charlatan. Maybe this will pacify Ray, but the chances are that he will want to try another one. He is very concerned that Rachel may be somewhere out there, trying to make contact with him. I still think that, if indeed such things are possible, she will send a sign of her own accord, without outside intervention.

Now the month of August is drawing nearer to a close and there is a distinct change in the weather. The nights are closing in and lots of things in the garden are beginning to flag. It all seems to have happened in the space of a week or is it just my imagination?

The fierce headaches of the past week seem to have abated somewhat but I cannot drum up any enthusiasm for anything. Even the garden, which initially gave me some comfort, has lost its attraction now. I know that I am coming across as a real pain and nobody wants to put up with a long face forever. There is a limit to people's patience and sympathy. I know this but it doesn't help and feel too beaten down to pull myself out of this despair. I won't consult a doctor as I don't want to be given anti-depressants. Eventually they would have to stop and would only mask the pain, not remove it. Better to try and face up to life as it is going to be from now onwards. Had Rachel's death been any other than the kind it was, there would be less excuse for my behaviour. However, under the circumstances, it is impossible to try and get on with life because the trial is still to be faced. It is only about eight weeks away now.

Having spoken with Vanda in the morning about the non-appearance of the police for at least six weeks, I arrive home to find one of them at the door. Ray is at work and, on these occasions, I feel more relaxed and freer to speak. I am always on edge when Ray is present during these meetings as his behaviour can be unpredictable. This may be understandable, but the police are only doing a job. They are our only hope for justice (of a sort) and so I see no point in falling out with them. Previously, Ray has become very angry and confrontational and this is no help whatsoever. Not to them, not to him and certainly not to me.

I am handed a letter from the Chief Constable. This refers to a burglary which took place at our home back in May and it explains the outcome of the ensuing court case. The felon has pleaded guilty and been given a two-year sentence. This is a big relief to me as it means that Ray will not now have to attend court and give evidence against the thief. There is no mention, however, of any of the stolen goods being recovered. More recently, Mark's new flat has been burgled but nobody has been apprehended for that particularly mean and nasty theft. How anyone could take away the only things that are keeping that boy sane (his PlayStation, music centre, CDs and DVDs) is beyond comprehension. At the same time, they have taken away his confidence too and he is left feeling afraid. Just as despicable was the person who stole a beautiful floral basket from Rachel's graveside. People who steal from the living are one thing but robbing the dead is something else and I found it soul-destroying at the time.

But I know that the letter from the Chief Constable is a mere formality. There will be other issues raised, as there have been on all other visits, I am certain of that. I am proved right when, after skirting around various bits of trivia, I am given an update on the current situation. At least, as much of an update as I am going to get!

The latest worry is that Michael Little has now dismissed his lawyers and engaged another firm to act for him. This could well mean the trial will not now go ahead in October after all. It is possible, and highly likely, that this new crowd will ask the judge for more time to get their case together. It could also mean that they will not retain the same defence lawyer and I have mixed feelings on that.

I am told that my fears may be unfounded, that the judge could still insist on the trial going ahead on the set date, especially since this has happened at such a late stage in the proceedings. The police have heard nothing from the Crown Prosecution Service to say otherwise but I remain unconvinced. It seems like a severe blow and a definite setback because I am looking to nothing now except October. Perhaps the trial will not even take place this year, so our agony will be prolonged even further.

The other disturbing piece of news is that the potential witness Little has named still refuses to co-operate with the prosecution. The police don't seem unduly concerned by his reluctance to help them and have decided to discount him as a witness. I am told that the case against Little is so overwhelming that they know he alone committed the crime. I have to believe this but am beginning to doubt these reassurances more and more, and to be terrified of some legal loophole or some miscarriage of justice which will allow this filthy pig to go free. Again, I am desperate to know everything that the police will be using in evidence but am resigned to the fact that I must wait until the trial comes around.

I voice some of these fears to my friendly copper and he tries to explain away my doubts. The fact is, the longer he is on remand, the less he will serve of his sentence in a real prison. Meanwhile, he is allowed to wear his own clothes, and no doubt has lots of privileges and support. The true facts of what he did have yet to be revealed, so for now his credibility remains intact. It seems his mother is the only one of his family standing by him and is still in contact. I wonder, but don't ask, exactly where he is incarcerated at the moment, if and how visitors are able to see him if the jail is some distance away. I am incensed to think that they may be given travel permits or hand-outs at the expense of the tax-payer. I have no doubt that, wherever he is, he is living a far superior life to that which he had outside. Even if he is not, he is still alive, a joy which Rachel does not have.

The police involvement in the case is petering out now as the investigation has run its course. All that can be gathered has been, apart from tying up odds and ends. Unless something earth-shattering comes to light, they will be keeping a low profile. Their work is almost complete and it is just a case of waiting now. Waiting and hoping that the trial comes to pass in October. Whatever happens, I will be given some help beforehand regarding my statement and how to conduct myself in court. I also learn now that Mark, too, is to be a witness and I am very fearful for him. It all leaves me with the certainty that there is much more to this case than we know. There must be, since the police are so supremely confident. I can only hope that they have got it right and that the jury will be on our side.

Our friend and pastor, Father White, arrives unexpectedly this evening. He has had some memorial booklets printed for us all, containing the words he spoke at the funeral. We are very touched by this gesture and realise again just how much her death has affected him. He just can't make any sense of it and again asks us, 'But why did he kill her, do you know?' It is very difficult to give him answers, since the information we have, has been entrusted to us and we are not at liberty to impart it to anybody at this stage.

Only two people know what really happened that night; one is incapable of telling the truth and sadly the other is no longer able to speak. Luckily, we do not have to rely on the words of a murderer, nor do we have to give any credence to his far-fetched story. We have the wonder of modern-day technology to disprove all the lies that drip from his lips. This is our weapon and I thank God for it.

We have no doubt in our minds that Rachel was abducted, though the means have not yet been made clear to us, and that Little's sole intention was to have sex with her, with or without her consent. We know that *did* happen and the chances are high that it occurred post-mortem. How can we tell a priest that? How can we tell him that we know Rachel was trying to flee when he stabbed her in her back? What good would it do him to know that, even as she lay there dying, this vile brute continued to stab her many more times, in the neck and the chest? Even Ray doesn't fully comprehend yet that this is what happened. That is how our lovely, innocent girl's life came to an end – totally desecrated in a filthy hovel.

Why did he kill her? Probably because she could identify him or perhaps because he is so evil that he enjoyed doing it. I am quite certain that he doesn't feel remorse, since by now he has convinced himself that it wasn't his fault but hers.

I am getting anxious that now, after six months, Rachel still has no headstone marking her place of rest. Back in February, hers was almost the first new grave in the allotted area but now the place is nearly full. Most of the graves do have stones and I think the time has come to do something about it. I cannot do this alone since all the family's views and ideas must be taken into account. In theory, so should

Mark's but I know he will be happy with our decision when it is finally made. Above all, I want Rachel's stone to be unique and totally different to any other in the cemetery. It isn't a thing I ever discussed with her but feel I do know her tastes quite well. She was a very 'girly' girl and so I am in favour of a pink marble headstone, simple and minimal, but one which will make a statement. She deserves and therefore will have nothing but the best. I hope it will be something that people will look at and remember her by. I hope also that it will be in place before the end of the year. Once that happens, it will be another milestone and yet another reminder that she is no longer with us.

This month is almost over and I see changes all around me. The days are becoming autumnal; they match my mood. Our only son will reach his 29th birthday tomorrow and I feel I must make some small effort on his behalf. It is not fair to expect him to give up on life and I hope that he will be able to go out and at least try to enjoy himself. I think that, to a point, he has blocked out of his mind what happened to Rachel, though I know deep down he is devastated. He shies away whenever I broach the subject and is still spending many hours alone in his room or on the computer.

Since the latest visit from the police, I am unable to put out of my mind what was discussed. I am tormenting myself more and more by trying to imagine what happened to Rachel on that night. Although it would not help the situation one jot, I am desperate to know the probable scenario and *now*, not at the trial. It is becoming an obsession and I want to talk about nothing else but find willing ears few and far between. My main sounding board continues to be Vanda, but even she, I feel, is becoming weary of my constant harping on about it. It is all getting to her now in the worst possible way and it is not helping her health at all.

Kerry, I know, is also becoming more and more irritated with my ramblings on the occasions when she rings our house. Living so far away and for such a long time, she has no real concept of how it is here for us, nor did she know Rachel as well as the rest of the family. It would upset her, no doubt, to know that there have been times recently when I feel very let down by her. I can't explain this and know that I am not being strictly fair to her. She has many problems of her own to which I have given little thought this year. How, then, can I expect more from her? She is doing her best and I can ask no more than that.

Apart from Ray, my remaining three children are all that I have really. There are no surviving parents and I have few relatives, either in this town or anywhere else. Ray is luckier and, in some ways, I envy the fact that he has a large and extended family all over the world. It is from this family that he is able to draw much comfort and they have been a great support to him during this terrible time. They are very concerned about him and keep in constant touch, which helps him.

It is good for me, therefore, to receive a call from our friend John Murray who, probably without knowing it, helped me a great deal. Speaking from experience, he was able to dispel a lot of my self-doubt and fear, to make me feel that I am not abnormal in my present way of thinking, nor am I without hope. I have come to the conclusion that it is far easier to discuss some things with an outsider than it is with those who are close to you. Could this be why Ray seems happier to talk to his distant family than to me?

I am given another little boost this week when I am told by a person I have never met before that I am very brave. Am I? I never think of myself as being so but coming from a stranger it was not only surprising but very heartening. This is the first time since the very early days that anyone has paid me a compliment and it lifts my spirits, though not for long. No matter how many times I tell myself that I will make greater efforts to pull myself up out of this despondency, I am still finding it impossible to do so. On the rare occasions when Ray and I have been able to voice a few of our opinions, when our thoughts have seemed parallel, the next day invariably shows nothing has changed. It is becoming very frightening as we drift further apart, each of us trapped in our own misery, each of us afraid or unwilling to say what we really feel. I worry about the future, after the trial is over and what direction our lives will take then. I cannot let it all end like this, not after 40 years and all that we have endured together during those years.

Some of these years I had already written about in a previous diary, when things seemed as bad as they could be. I know now that everything is relative and that nothing could compare to this present hell. My only consolation is that, having read accounts of others who have lost a child to murder, their experiences in the aftermath are all similar to ours. Their doubts, fears and anger, the fragmentation of their family and in some cases the collapse of their marriage. I am determined that this will not happen in our case, that we will survive and become stronger through it. If the words I write will help another unfortunate family who have suffered a fate such as ours, then Rachel's death will not have been entirely in vain. I only wish I could have found someone to talk to from the beginning, someone who had experienced a similar tragedy and who could have told me how it would be. Perhaps then I would be handling this far better than I am.

And so the month of August draws to a close. Should the trial go ahead on 13 October, that leaves only six weeks of wondering and worrying. Not knowing how these things proceed, I am unsure as to what will happen. Does the fact that there has been no further police visits mean that the trial will go ahead, despite Michael Little's last-minute change of lawyer? I fully expect that, much nearer the date, the police will inform us that extra time has been requested. Nothing will surprise me, so, for the moment, I am basing my life around the original date. If only we knew a bit more of what really happened and what actual evidence there is to support the prosecution case. Will we ever know the truth?

I read through my diary and come to the conclusion that anyone else who reads it would consider it very one-sided and self-centred. I make no excuses for this since it is, essentially, *my* story. It is my own thoughts and feelings since this all occurred. Should Ray or any of my three remaining children wish to put their own thoughts in writing at some stage, then they must do so. These are mine, for what they are worth.

I have tried very hard over the past few days to make life more easy but the stifling atmosphere prevails. Is it me? Am I not trying hard enough to smooth the way? Whenever I think that things seem a little better between Ray and me, a new day dawns and we are back to where we were. I am so very tired, both physically and mentally, and I have the need to talk. Why can't we, I wonder? Is it that we are both so destroyed and beaten down by all of this that we are each our own worst enemy? It is just impossible when I see Ray in a world of his own, remembering nothing he is told and taking nothing in. I could easily be like this myself, but I must make the effort to keep going despite everything. Vanda needs some help most days and, while I am here, I will give it to her. By doing so, this does not mean that thoughts of Rachel don't overwhelm me too at all times. I just have to be realistic and try to get on with a life of sorts.

I worry constantly that our moods are upsetting John. Small wonder he is talking of buying his own place and moving out. What is going to happen to us after the trial, when we have no further excuses? Was our marriage in such a state that the loss of Rachel has tipped it over the edge? I really didn't think so before this happened but maybe I was blinkered and 40 years together counted for nothing much. Perhaps we weren't as rock solid as I thought we were.

I think I have done my best to be as good a wife and mother as I could during these years and that I have been as supportive as the next in times of trouble, but perhaps my best hasn't been good enough. There is no doubt that Ray has always been a good husband and father but we are two utterly different personalities. He has no problems with doing his own thing from time to time, whereas I have to put everyone else's needs before my own. Maybe I have been wrong from the start and I must now try to do what I want to once in a while. I realise that nobody will think any the worse of me for doing so but the habits of a lifetime are very hard to break. This tragedy has done little to change me and

I am still trying to continue as normal, without success it seems. Eventually, something will have to give and I feel I am heading for a fall of monumental proportions.

Saturday, 30 August 2003

I spend the afternoon with Vanda and, on returning home, feel as bad as ever. My mood is black and I have little to say to Ray. I go into the garden and find, to my absolute dismay, that our neighbour has trimmed down the hedge between our two houses and, at the same time, has decimated a Christmas fir tree on our side to be level with the hedge. I had been growing the tree for seven years. I am furiously angry and completely gutted because it had reached about 8ft in height and was impossible to miss. My intention had been to decorate this tree with outdoor lights at the New Year, for the anniversary of Rachel's death. It seems like, in felling the tree, he has struck another blow against her, as it means one more thing that I cannot do for her. I know I am rapidly approaching the end of my tether.

The evening drags on with neither of us saying very much and, since there is nothing better to do, I go up to bed at around 9.30pm. Ray stays downstairs. I try very hard to sleep but cannot, even though I am desperately tired. Things are going round and round in my head – the hopelessness of the situation, the interminable silences, which are my fault as much as Ray's, and the final straw of Rachel's tree being hewn.

Suddenly and without reason, I am up and dressed and I go downstairs with the intention of getting out of the house – out of this atmosphere and away. Ray is sitting in silence in the back lounge but comes out into the kitchen, perhaps because he hears me. He asks where I am going and seems slightly taken aback when I say, 'Out,' as it is now around 11pm and normally I never go anywhere at night. He makes no effort to stop me and I don't expect or want him to. Right now, I have no idea where I will go but know that I will explode if I remain in this house one moment longer. I lock the door behind me and walk off into the night, carrying only my handbag.

I keep walking and thinking, wondering where I should go but quite determined not to go to anyone with whom I am acquainted. I am on my own – I have left for the sake of my sanity and wish to involve nobody else.

I carry on towards the city centre, stopping once to withdraw some cash from an ATM. I pass within yards of Vanda's house and for one fleeting moment consider going there. I know she will not be in bed as she too is plagued with insomnia, but it would be unfair of me to bring her into this. I feel very rational and, in a way, quite exhilarated to be free. I am thinking only of myself and don't even consider that I may be acting irresponsibly by walking out.

There are one or two scary moments, since it is quite late in the evening and there is, as always, an element of rowdy and inebriated folk around, this being a Saturday night. I know that I don't want to stay on the streets all night so, perhaps subconsciously, I find myself heading for a hotel near the city centre. I have money and I have my credit cards. Now all I need is the courage to walk through the door and ask for a room.

It turns out to be so easy and not one person gives me a second glance. It is as if it is quite normal for an elderly lady to walk in off the streets without car or luggage, seeking sanctuary for the night! I am seen to without delay and lock myself in the room. I feel very safe in this little haven and try to settle down for the night. Once again, however, sleep eludes me. I think I am too keyed up at this stage, so I spend a restless few hours awaiting the dawn.

Although it is included in the price, I don't have breakfast, probably because I have no wish to be seen by anybody but also because my appetite has disappeared entirely. I wait until around 10am and then go down to the reception to hand in my room key. When I do so, for some reason I find myself asking if the room is available for a further two nights. When I am told it is, I book it and pay the receptionist with my credit card. Following this, I leave for the day.

I know that, if I am to remain at the hotel, I will need a few personal things — toiletries, a nightgown perhaps and some reading material. I decide to walk towards the city and spend a not-unpleasant day, taking in a market/car boot sale and browsing through some of the shops in the town. I don't imagine for one minute that anyone will be out looking for me — not yet and probably not at all — but I keep a sharp lookout nevertheless. I don't want to be seen by anybody who knows me. I am not ready for confrontation at the moment.

Because I am so unused to walking very far nowadays, I am extremely tired by early evening and wish only to get back to my safe little room at the hotel. I return with the bits and pieces I have purchased and manage to get inside undetected. It feels very good to be there all on my own and I am beginning to find some peace of mind. It doesn't enter my head that people may be worried about me. I just assume that they know I am a sensible person and unlikely to come to harm.

I have a luxurious bath and settle down to do a bit of reading and to think about where I will spend the next day. I am very tired now, but quite relaxed and in control of myself. The flight from home and the walking have taken their toll and by 9pm I am in bed. I sleep well for the first time in eight months, and only wake at 6am the following morning. Again I forego breakfast, although I haven't eaten since Saturday and it is now Monday. I am not hungry, though, and feel beyond eating. I leave the hotel by 9am and set off walking towards the city centre, stopping along the way to draw out some more money. The weather is warm and I feel a little out-of-place in my trousers and woollen jacket but nobody shows any untoward interest in me.

I decide I will take a bus into York and spend the day there. I want to get out of this town and don't want to risk running into anyone who knows me here. I find out the times of buses and sit in the station buffet until 10am, when I leave for York. The journey is pleasant, the passengers few and I spend an agreeable day on my own. There is one bad moment during the early afternoon, when my lack of food catches up with me and I feel as though I'm about to faint. God forbid I should end up in the hospital, so I make myself have a sandwich and afterwards I feel all right again. It feels good to browse around alone and I buy a few little trinkets to take home for the family. As ever, they are all in my thoughts, but I am not worrying about them. I don't even consider that they might be worrying about me, not at this stage anyway.

After a long and tiring day, I am happy to get back to the hotel again and the peaceful silence of my room. Nobody is looking out for me, so obviously my disappearance has so far gone unreported. This night I truly am exhausted and am really winding down by now. After a nice long soak, I am in bed by 8pm. I have another reasonable night's sleep and awaken early the next morning. As before, I do not attend breakfast and leave at 9am to walk into the city centre. The walking is becoming easier as I get used to it and I make the journey quite quickly. Once more I find myself in the station buffet for a time and I have an energy drink to keep me going for the day. I had decided the previous evening that I would head out to Beverley and spend a few hours there, so I already know when and from where the bus will leave.

It's another gloriously warm day and quite an enjoyable one. I look around the shops, buy a few oddments and sit and watch the world go by. I know that my time away is drawing to a close and I must return home at some stage today. It was always my intention to do so and I feel recharged and ready to face up to things now. I have done a lot of thinking and perhaps seen the error of my ways. I have come to the conclusion that I have been so full of my own pain and suffering that I have paid little attention to anyone else's. We are all so distraught by the loss of Rachel, each in our own way, so why should I, her mother, feel it any more than anyone else?

I arrive back in Hull city centre in the early evening and begin to feel slightly nervous for the first time since I walked out of the house. I have not seen a newspaper since I left home, nor the news, so have no idea if I may have been reported missing. However, nobody gives me a second look when I get on the bus, so I assume I must have remained out of the news during my absence. I imagine that, even if Ray has reported me as a missing person, he would not do so until today at the earliest, so I can be home again before any fuss is made. How wrong I am ...

The street and the house seem strangely quiet when I let myself in and it's as if nobody is at home. Then Ray appears from somewhere and casually asks how I am feeling. It is very odd to be back home and feels as if I have been away for a long, long time. I feel completely in control of myself and somewhat defiant, especially when I learn that the whole world and his mother have been searching for me from day one. This comes as a shock and annoys me a little, though strangely enough it doesn't bother me, as such publicity would have done once upon a time.

Ray is quite angry with me and considers my behaviour irresponsible but, after some discussion, we begin to see each other's point of view and call an uneasy truce. I don't know what is going to happen to us in the future but at least now we are talking. We are speaking of our doubts and fears, as we should have done months ago. I have no regrets that I bolted, nor does it bother me that people were looking for me. I don't even care that the police became involved. I just know that I had to go and I feel all the better for it now.

I have a couple of drinks and a bath, after which I am very tired and so decide to retire for the night. Ray makes and takes several telephone calls and I am told that the police will be arriving in the morning to speak to me. Well, who cares? My son arrives home and seems very happy to see me, as well as somewhat relieved, I think.

Sleep does not come easily and I am up again by 3.30am and unable to rest for the remainder of the night. There are lots more phone calls this morning from family and friends who were concerned about me, and this is quite surprising. Until now, I thought that everybody just saw me as someone in the background who kept things going. It seems I was wrong all along.

Ray and John are very attentive towards me today, as are the police when they arrive. Everybody seems to be treating me like some sort of an invalid who is on the verge of a breakdown. This is so untrue. I am still the same, strong woman underneath but I had gone as far as I could go. I know now that I can see this thing through. I know what I have to do and I will do it, to see that my family survives this most terrible of tragedies.

I am very touched that both Ray and John have gone out and bought me little gifts, that messages of support came via friends and neighbours, all happy that I am back home again. Perhaps they do care after all? Ray is having a few days off work and we go off on our own once or twice. We both open up about our thoughts on Rachel, and I, at least, feel better for it. Ray is worried about me and I am worried about him, so we will have to take care of each other.

We are drawn one day, for the first time ever, to a village only seven or eight miles away and while there we visit an ancient church and graveyard. In this place, we spot the grave of a child who died in the 1800s and her epitaph could have been written for Rachel's headstone. We know at once that it is what we have been looking for and wonder if Rachel herself sent us there to find it. We spend a pleasant few hours in this lovely little village and are surprised that we never knew of its existence before. I think that we are both beginning to recharge our batteries, though we are very tired, both physically and emotionally.

Tonight I have a few words with Kerry, who I suspect was as annoyed as she was worried when I disappeared. I have decided to keep all of my conversations neutral until after the trial, both with her and with Vanda. Maybe I have been unfair to both of them with my constant harping on about the situation. I have not spoken to Vanda since I returned but will see her on 7 September, her 35th birthday.

After outings on two consecutive days, Ray and I are weary. I feel as if I have run a marathon and now need to rest. I imagine this is a result of the past week and all that has occurred since then.

We visit Vanda on her birthday and take her a few gifts. I detect a slight coolness in her manner towards me and can understand why. I suppose she thought that I would get in touch with her above all people while I was away, but I couldn't do that to her. I couldn't put the responsibility on her shoulders by telling her not to let anyone know where I was. I simply had to be out of reach for a while and entirely on my own. Hopefully in time she will realise my reasoning behind all of this.

Ray is back at work this Monday morning and I speak with Vanda on the telephone. She seems OK and thanks us for the birthday presents. She is curious as to where I hid myself for three days but I am not ready to tell her yet. She will know soon enough and we will laugh about it all at some later date.

Ray and I do some work together in the garden and visit the cemetery. I find it quite amusing to learn that the police were lurking there while I was away, in the hope that I would turn up at some stage!

After eight months of doing only the minimum of chores around the house, I decide to have a blitz on the housework. It is still a great effort to do anything and I am very tired, but I *am* trying.

It seems that the trial will indeed begin on 13 October, which leaves us less than five weeks. I refuse to even think about it because, when I do, I become seriously afraid. I am assured by the police that there is no way that Rachel's name can or will be dragged through the mud, but that is still my biggest fear. That and having to listen to what that hateful pig did to her. My child's terror does not bear thinking of. Ray tells me he has a permanent knot in his stomach and is constantly on edge. He will need my strength more than ever in the weeks to come, and I shall need his. Thank God there are so many people behind us in all this, all wanting to see justice done, rooting for us. I am especially glad that Kerry will be here with us for at least some of the trial, and that Ray's only brother is to make the journey from Ireland. I know that he will be a great source of comfort and support to Ray and that's what he will need, what we will all need.

I read yesterday that a couple whose daughter was murdered four years ago are to divorce, even though the wife is about to give birth again. Reading her words struck a note with me and I could empathise with each of them. Only those who have suffered such a loss can understand the feelings and emotions one goes through, how a family can be destroyed. It is quite frightening to read also that statistics show 98 per cent of couples separate after such an event. I am very determined that Ray and I are going to be in the two per cent who do not.

Tuesday, 9 September 2003

A very poignant day, since it's the 17th anniversary of the death of my mother – a grandmother who Rachel never really got the chance to know, no more than she did her paternal granny in Ireland. Both are now long gone and perhaps it's as well, for how could they have endured knowing what happened to her? For our sakes, however, I have wished many times over these past months for our own parents' presence and comfort in these terrible times.

I need to go out in the car, the first time I have driven in more than ten days. I am a little wary because I feel quite spaced out, not entirely with it. While on my travels, I am dealt another body blow, this being the first day of the new term after the summer break. How heart-rending to see all the children in their new uniforms, full of exuberance and the joy of life. I cannot help but see Rachel in each one of them and remember her first days at St Vincent's and then St

Mary's. Such happy days and how were we to know they would be cut so cruelly short? It is hard not to feel bitter and to wish with all my heart that I could turn back the hands of time, just to see her once more and to hear her voice, but that can never be. I feel very sad today and am finding it hard to hold back the tears but I must bear up, if only for Ray's sake. I can't upset or worry him any more by giving in to my own feelings. He has enough to cope with, I know that now.

Ray has made an appointment to have a one-to-one with a clairvoyant tomorrow evening. I still have the same attitude towards this school of thought but, if it will give Ray some comfort, then so be it. I only hope it doesn't upset him in any way when the time comes. At the very least, it will be an interesting exercise and one that I feel he must lay to rest sooner rather than later.

My boss telephones me this evening and we have a nice long chat. We keep the conversation neutral and she asks nothing of me, only listens. As a trained nurse, she has some concept of psychological problems and I take comfort from our talk. Happily, she doesn't mention work, knowing I'm sure that it is the least of my worries at present. The thought of ever returning fills me with dread – I don't know if I could cope with it again.

We discuss the fact that none of us has really called upon medical intervention so far, be it in the form of counselling or medication. She suggests that now might be the time to visit our GP and ask for help in these last weeks leading up to the trial. I can see the wisdom of her words and know that it would not be an admission of failure to cope, but I am still wary of doing so. My pride tells me not to give in but common sense tells me otherwise. I think perhaps I am embarrassed to take that final step of entering the surgery and admitting defeat. Is this a foolish attitude I wonder? I do agree, however, to allow her to contact on my behalf an ex-colleague who is a trained clinical psychiatric nurse and counsellor. In the past, when my youngest brother died in terrible circumstances, this man was a great help to me, so perhaps he will be again. I will have no problem in just talking with him, nor do I think would Ray. I await a call to arrange a meeting, initially for myself but perhaps for Ray too at some stage. God help us that we should ever have to resort to such tactics, but maybe there comes a time when it is no longer possible to go it alone and maybe that time is now.

I have not spoken to any of Ray's family for quite some time and I wonder what they really think of my little rebellion. I imagine that they consider I let Ray down badly but I may be wrong again. His oldest sister sent an email from America voicing the opinion that I am probably suffering from depression. This is true, since obviously we all must be, but it was not depression that drove me away from home. I am still strong and my general attitude has not changed in the past eight months. I can see this thing through. I was always capable of doing so – all it needed was for us to pull together rather than against each other. Both of us and yet neither of us have been at fault up until now and my going away just brought about a climax. I wish that people could understand that.

Ray's greatest mistake was to let his family think, during his conversations with them, that he was doing fine which was, and continues to be, far from the truth. It has been impossible for me to get across to them that it is only an act on Ray's part and that, once off the phone, he reverts back to how he has been since all this started. It is understandable that they do not take my words seriously but, at the same time, it is very frustrating. Maybe if they were here with us they would come to realise just how terribly he is suffering and how hard each day is for him to get through. I have seen his grief from the very beginning. I have lived with it until the point came when I could cope with it no longer. I hope that at some stage they will come to understand that and will then see that it was this, more than depression, which made me walk out that night.

Ray and I are beginning to talk more and more, even though John does not involve himself in our conversations. He still will not speak of Rachel and seems to be masking his true feelings by going out and drinking. That, and his spending many hours alone upstairs, tells me he is badly affected and this is his way of dealing with things. He is, in that respect, much the same as the rest of this family. We all tend to keep our feelings hidden. From the day that Rachel went missing, we have all tried to keep a dignified front and we continue to do so even now. Because of this, people might be forgiven for thinking that we are somehow superhuman and more capable than most of coping with our loss – an assumption that would be totally wrong. This event has destroyed us as a family in just the same way as it would a family who made a song and dance about it. We are in a no-win situation. We put on a brave face to the world and are considered to be getting over it, or we tell it how it really is and folk very quickly begin to tire of our misery.

I did a lot of people-watching during my three days away and began to realise that one never knows what others have going on in their lives. I may be walking along the street and, unless I were known to you, you would not have a clue as to my suffering and the same could be said of many others. This struck home today when I received a short letter from an ex-workmate who I didn't know very well. At the time, I thought her a nice, quiet woman, slightly nervous in her demeanour, who kept herself very much to herself. I knew that she had two sons but she now tells me that she also had a young daughter whom she lost some years ago, so she does have some idea of what we are going through. I feel very bad that I didn't take the time to speak to her more than I did. I realise now why she seemed to be apart from the rest of us in the office and how tormented she must have been, unable to speak about her lost child. She offers some support and comfort and I determine to send her a reply and my thanks for her concern.

It has been very hard to get myself motivated since I came back home, mainly due to the exhaustion I feel from the moment I arise each morning. In reality, there is little that I am forced to do, apart from the minimum of housework and cooking, but I feel guilty that I have no enthusiasm for that even. If I let myself think of the trial, I become very frightened, even terrified, so I resolve not to think about it. To a point, I enjoy the solitude of being alone here in the house but I miss Ray when he is at work and feel insecure until he returns. I am beginning to fear leaving the house on my own, partly due to my aversion to bumping into folk who know me. I imagine that even strangers now recognise my face and are pointing a finger at me. I wonder if this is some kind of phobia, am I losing control?

In some ways, it might be good to have people around me but, at the same time, I don't want anyone apart from my immediate family. I am told these are all stages of the natural process of grieving but I am not convinced. Perhaps I really am going mad and am not the strong person I thought I was. Maybe after the trial, when at least some of the truth is told, things will become a little better. It should then be possible to discuss things with friends and relations, without fear of jeopardising the case. The hardest part now is not being able to breathe a word to anyone about what happened to Rachel that night, when all we want to do is talk about it. Having to keep what little information we are privy to a secret is soul-destroying and is killing us little by little each day.

This is the evening that Ray is to visit the clairvoyant and he arrives home early to wash and change out of his working clothes. He is very nervous and unsure what to expect. I too am nervous, worried and apprehensive, both for him and myself. It is quite a long drive from our home to her place and I am afraid of him having to make the return journey in what could be a distraught state. However, I choose not to accompany him.

When Ray gets home a couple of hours later, he seems very quiet and somewhat bemused. I give him a few moments and then ask him what it was like. 'Weird,' he replies, and then goes upstairs. He seems rather shaken by the experience, so I give him time to unwind before we sit down together. Our Catholic faith tells us that we should pay no heed to spiritualism etc. and, as I have said previously, we are not the sort of people who would have taken any notice of it before all this occurred. However, the events of the last eight months have changed us entirely and, like others before us, we are now clutching at any straw which may lead us to Rachel, that may show us she is indeed out there somewhere.

What Ray tells me, and what we then hear on the tape he

was given afterwards, certainly gives one pause for thought. The facts that she didn't ask his name prior to his appointment, that she lives so far from our area, and even that Ray is not as easily recognisable as I may be, all lead me to believe that this lady could not possibly have found out so much about him. She couldn't have known the many intimate things about him, names, events from his past which have never been made known, and so I come to the conclusion that she is no charlatan.

Then there's the part on the tape when this lady becomes very distressed. Ray tells me she was almost fainting and he became concerned for her. She then asks him, 'Was your daughter murdered?' and repeats this a few times. She turns off the tape at this point so I must rely on Ray's version of what was said afterwards. Perhaps she had recognised him – who can say – but he is comforted that Rachel *is* out there and looking over us, while at the same time remaining sceptical. It leaves me in a strange state of mind and I listen to the tape repeatedly. I am cold and shivering and cannot sleep at all, with everything going through my head. Maybe the oddest thing about it all is that the woman refused to take any payment for her services. She tells Ray that she has done it for Rachel, so maybe she did genuinely see something out there. I don't know what to think but know that the idea of consulting the woman myself is now a distinct possibility.

Ray speaks to Kerry on the telephone about his experience and she immediately bursts into tears. She believes it all implicitly and is comforted. Vanda is shaken when she hears what transpired and decides that she will make an appointment to see the woman at the first opportunity.

Writing this, it seems absurd that we – a sensible, rational family – can be so excited by what most people would consider a load of garbage. I can only reiterate that we are clutching at straws because we so need to know there is something in the afterlife and that one day we will see Rachel again. That she is waiting for us somewhere but until that day comes perhaps it is only natural that those left behind want some tangible evidence that this is so. I truly cannot say.

Even though it is now mid-September, the weather continues to be brilliant. Only the early darkness tells one that it is autumn and not the height of summer. The garden is fading somewhat but there is still a lot of colour out there. Rachel's roses continue to bloom and I visit her corner of the garden many times each day. This is where I feel she is and her wind chime always seems to tinkle when I approach, even on the stillest of days. My heart almost breaks each time this happens because I don't want to feel her presence in this way. I want to see her in reality, to touch her and to laugh with her. Oh God, why did You take her away from us? How are we to go on without her for the rest of our lives? The pain is so very physical and at times almost impossible to bear. It is hard to even appreciate that there are three other children and three grandchildren left behind. Nothing can compensate for the loss of one of them.

I am becoming very selfish in my grief. There are times in the cemetery when other bereaved parents approach us, speaking of their own loss and identifying with us. Their children, too, had been young and their deaths tragic, yet I feel that they bear no comparison to Rachel's, simply because she was murdered and they were not. I feel greatly for them all and their loss, and their pain is no less than ours, but there is a subtle difference.

In the majority of deaths, there is shock, anger and devastation. Then there is the burial, usually quite quickly afterwards, the initial grieving and then comes the time to try and start living again. In our case, and similar ones, none of that happened. We had a month of not knowing, another month before we could lay Rachel to rest, the inability to see her and say our last goodbyes, the ongoing police case and now the long wait for the trial. Our lives continue to be on hold and, after all these months, there is still no closure for us. There can be no closure, only the learning to live with this thing. Meanwhile, we worry constantly about the impending trial, the renewed publicity which will undoubtedly ensue, and the greatest fear of all — will, by some quirk of fate, the odious beast walk free?

Our good friend and pastor Father White has been in Ireland for almost a month, taking a much needed rest after this traumatic year. He is due home at the weekend and we look forward to seeing him. Ray and I are getting along much better since my return. We are often quiet with each other but in a totally different way to how we were before I went. Occasionally, I can even get a little lift and have positive thoughts about the future but then guilt kicks in and I wonder how I can be so disloyal to Rachel that I could ever think of the future without her. Ray has similar thoughts of guilt and disloyalty but, in his case, he doesn't ever feel happy enough to think of the future. I fear that, despite my efforts to keep buoyant for his sake, it is not working. He continues to feel morose and has physical and mental symptoms hanging over him much of the time.

We meet up with my brother and his wife in the cemetery and she is shocked by my appearance. I know that I have lost almost a stone and a half in weight. My hair has grown long and out of shape and I look like a completely different person to the one I was eight months ago. To my shame, I have also taken up smoking again and can't seem to even consider going to bed at night without at least one alcoholic drink inside me. What would Rachel think of it all, I wonder, and conclude that she would not want us acting in the way we all are, but it is so monstrously hard to behave any differently.

Saturday, 13 September 2003

A glorious day and one we have made plans for. Vanda remains ill and tires very easily, so she is unable to walk or even tolerate car journeys very well. However, she expresses a desire to visit a World War II museum about an hour's drive from our home. Eden Camp is a remarkable place which we have visited before – an authentic PoW camp where Italian prisoners were held, set in the North Yorkshire moors, a beautiful part of the country. We are happy to go, although it will be poignant as Rachel was always with us in the past. Still, we cannot go through life avoiding places just because of this, so we set off in as good cheer as we can muster.

The day goes well enough and four hours pass quickly before we need to leave for home. Vanda is exhausted as walking is a great effort for her and we want only to get her home and settled for the evening. We stop en route to do some shopping for her and for us. I am still not feeling up to the almost daily visits I used to make to her place before my three days adrift from the family. This, then, is a rare opportunity to stock up on supplies until such time as I get back into a more normal routine.

I still feel that my confidence is ebbing away and I am almost afraid to go anywhere on my own nowadays. I scurry in and out of the house, try to peg out the laundry without being seen by my neighbours and the mere sound of the telephone fills me with dread. I only feel safe when Ray or John are in the house or are with me. What is happening to me? I visited my doctor last week for the first time since February and he prescribed some sort of anti-depressants. However, I still haven't had the prescription filled. I am afraid to become reliant on anything, knowing that, at some point in the future, I will have to stop taking them and face reality.

We arrive home rather tired following our brief sojourn and feel quite certain that this is the night that Father White will surely call in to see us. I go into the garden to tend my hanging baskets and hear Ray welcoming someone to the house. I assume it is Father White as we have so few visitors but am surprised to see Father Gerard, a priest from our own local parish church, sitting there. We know him only slightly as we continue to attend St Vincent's, which is Father White's parish.

Father Gerard has come to offer his support at the trial as a friend, but also because, as an ex-prison chaplain, he has some experience in these matters. It is slightly awkward because we are expecting Father White to arrive at any moment, who has also vowed to be in court with us every day. John, our son, is also due in from work soon and, between us, we are attempting to cook a meal for him and entertain Father

Gerard while awaiting Father White's arrival. Meanwhile, unbeknown to me, Ray has spotted Father White outside our house in his car and tells him Father Gerard is there. Father White decides to wait outside until he leaves. The only reason for this is that we know Father White on a more personal level and have been able to tell him some aspects of the coming court case, so we want to talk to him in confidence. Seeing these words now makes it all seem underhand and rather mean, but it wasn't like that at all.

Father Gerard is in great form and stays for about two hours. John arrives home and eats his meal and Ray, still without my knowledge, keeps going in and out of the house through the kitchen to update Father White, who is still sitting outside in his car. Eventually, around 8.30pm, he decides to wait no longer and comes to our door. I have given up on him coming and so I am surprised to see him but happy nevertheless. A little bit of banter ensues between the two priests and cups of tea are made, though Father Gerard refuses a second cup and leaves. Ray walks with him to the end of the drive. It is now around 9pm and dark outside. He tells the Father to take care and comes back inside.

After speaking with Father White for a few minutes, I go into the kitchen to look for something. Glancing into the hallway, I see and hear voices and activity at the end of our driveway but think only that it is teenagers passing by. John comes downstairs and also looks out, saying that something seems to be going on out there. He thinks someone is lying on the ground and he is concerned enough to go out and investigate. I take a peek from our doorstep. There are half-a-dozen youngsters, some on bicycles, and I see our neighbour bending over a prostrate figure on the pavement. John comes back in, looking rather shocked. He says it is Father Gerard and he has been hurt. I go to see what is happening and am greatly perturbed to see Father Gerard practically unconscious, his leg at a very strange angle and his head resting on a makeshift cushion. This cushion is soaked with blood, as is the pavement surrounding it. I am very alarmed and go in to tell Ray and Father White, both of whom are quite unaware anything has been going on.

We all go outside in a state of disbelief, taking care not to crowd around or add fuel to the situation. Father Gerard must have said his goodbye to Ray, stepped on to the footpath and then been knocked down by a motorbike being driven on the pavement. He wouldn't have expected it, though it is becoming a real problem along our road. This poor man came to us on an errand of mercy and for his pains is now lying severely injured and in great distress on our doorstep.

The police and ambulance arrive in quick succession and it is terrible to witness the agony of Father Gerard as they try to stabilise him. I realise at once the seriousness of his injuries. He has been hit first by the motorbike in his leg and has obviously gone down like a stone on to his head. He is a big man and well into his sixties. Working as I do in the medical sector, I am very worried and know that his leg is well and truly shattered, to say nothing of his head wound and the shock he is suffering.

The lad on the motorbike didn't even stop after he hit Father Gerard but the others at the scene are able to name him, so the police at least know who to look for and what his address is. Meanwhile, Father Collier – Father Gerard's counterpart – arrives, having been summoned, and he is extremely upset, as is Father White. I feel so very bad and guilty that this should have happened because of one man's kindness in thinking of us.

There is a lot of police activity now – floodlights, scene-of-crime officers, blue tape etc. Buses and cars slow down to rubberneck, along with numerous pedestrians. All of them know this house so well after the events of the last few months and God only knows what they think has happened here now. This house seems cursed, along with whoever dwells in or visits it. It's hard to imagine why, since a priest lived here before we bought it and Father White blessed it when we first moved in. Have we been such bad people that these terrible things are happening to us and because of us?

There is no opportunity to do anything tonight now, other than try to get over the shock of it all. Fathers Collier and White will follow the ambulance to the Infirmary to keep abreast of Father Gerard's condition. We don't even realise that we haven't eaten and daren't go to bed until we hear how he is. Father White calls back around 11.30pm and tells us that Father Gerard is in no grave danger at present. It is a great relief, but does nothing really to lift our demeanour.

On Sunday morning we go to Mass at 9am, having telephoned the hospital. The ward sister assures us that Father Gerard is fine but I am not convinced, knowing that this is a stock answer. Father White tells the congregation what has happened and also mentions where the accident occurred. I am horrified and imagine that everyone thinks it is the Moran family who are to blame for this latest incident. We hear that Father Gerard will spend three hours in surgery this morning to repair his broken tibia and fibula, but luckily he has suffered no permanent damage to his head. It certainly doesn't look like he will be able to officiate at his cousin's wedding over in

Ireland in the near future, as was his plan. Oh, God, where will it all end?

Apparently, the person who was suspected of being responsible for the accident actually came back to the scene last night and asked the police what had happened. The police arrested him and took him into custody. The worst thing is that, even if he were the guilty party, nothing much is likely to happen to him by way of punishment, despite the fact that several laws were broken and Father Gerard could have been killed.

The media are once again drawn to this address and Ray takes a call from one of my nephews. He has heard that there were police and an ambulance here last night and my sister is very worried that I am involved. It seems the general consensus is that I have finally lost the plot and done some harm to myself, especially since I ran away for those few days. They should know by now that I am a strong person and unlikely to step out of line again, even though I have no illusions about the tough times yet to come.

Father White visits us this Sunday evening and he and I have a little chat in the garden while Ray is at the cemetery. I think Father understands why I had to escape for those few days and can see that Ray and I seem more at peace with each other now. He gives us a Mass card from one of his own relatives in Tipperary, a lovely plaque with Rachel's name, its meaning and origin, and for me a book he bought while in Ireland. It is of this book that I will now write, since I read it in just a couple of hours and am full of it still.

The book is called *Rachel's Story* and is about a ten-year-old girl of that name who died in Ireland in 1999, under very sad circumstances. Her mother wanted to write it in her memory and as a permanent reminder of Rachel for her husband and three surviving children. From the minute I open this book, I am amazed at the similarities between this Rachel and our Rachel. There is even a facial likeness when she was that age – the big eyes, the lovely long hair, the dancing ability. It is all so familiar. Even though the similarity ends, since this young girl died of a sudden and largely unknown illness, the same pain and emotion is there for her family, as it presently is for us. This poor, poor mother expresses the very same feelings of anguish as I am doing now and her husband is suffering in much the same way as Ray is at the loss of a daughter.

Father White was totally correct in thinking that I would identify with every word in this book. It is the right time for me to be reading it and it seems like it was fate that made him buy it. I take some comfort from the final chapters, which tell of life after Rachel and I find some of the content quite extraordinary in its similarity to what we find happening. One such thing is Rachel's rainbow, which the mother sees as a sign of her presence here on earth. The sad thing about that is that we too have seen several rainbows since all this happened, despite there being practically no rain this year. Our granddaughter made me a cushion – a real work of art that is hard to describe, but which, among other things, plays the tune of 'Over the Rainbow'. Until now, that song held little meaning for me or for Rachel, but perhaps it should. Perhaps our Rachel is present in every rainbow? I find this book sad and poignant yet uplifting in a way and, for the first time since her death, I find myself shedding real tears for the loss of my beautiful daughter.

I am quite determined to write to this mother and I tell Father White of my intentions. His reply is that he was hoping

I would say that, so perhaps it is indeed God working His mysterious way, His wonders to perform?

I feel very uneasy today and want nothing other than to stay close to the house on my own. The trial begins in four weeks exactly and I am very afraid. I know the time will fly by now and I just want it to stand still. I sit in the garden bringing my diary up to date on a gloriously hot day – quite unlike mid-September. I do the very minimum amount of work in the house, prepare the simplest of meals and just iron one shirt at a time for John. How lazy I am becoming these days and how little can I be bothered with anything. Where has the livewire I once was disappeared to? I cannot imagine myself ever getting back on track. I feel that, if I could just sit and write and write all my thoughts down on paper, the pain would abate with each word.

I know that I must visit my GP again very soon, as my boss has called requesting that I submit a sick note for the first time. I see no way such a request would be denied but I feel unable to visit the surgery and face him. I have nothing to fear but fear itself, I tell myself.

One phone call today – it is the police and fills me with dread needlessly. One of our liaison team has heard about Father Gerard's accident and has just called to voice his concern. Nothing more than that. He tells me he is busy finalising the details for the start of the trial and asks me if I require security screens while I am giving evidence. I think not but know that I will need some support when the time comes. I am praying, above all, that I say the right thing and don't let Rachel down in any way. I owe it to her to do my very best. Perhaps at the end of the day I am more worried about giving evidence than I am willing to admit.

Tomorrow I will go to Vanda's house, where we are due a visit from our hairdresser. I feel ragged and dishevelled at present so maybe that will buck me up a bit. Despite my protestations to the contrary, I am now becoming obsessed with the desire to visit the clairvoyant before the trial starts. I need someone to tell me that things will be OK, that there is light at the end of the tunnel for us all, but my common sense tells me I am behaving irrationally, two-faced, even. Things are what we make them, not what anyone else tells us, and I must get a grip on myself.

I want nothing more now than to go to sleep and to wake up when all of this is over. I never realised before that I was such a coward, but, in my present thinking, I know that I am. Despite my renewed closeness and understanding with Ray, I don't feel able to divulge these terrifying thoughts to him. He is walking a very fine line right now and it would be unfair of me to worry him even further. Perhaps if Steve, the counsellor my boss had recommended, gets in touch I will be able to express my feelings more easily to him, get some reassurance from a trained person who is far removed from the case and from us. My nerves are in such a state today that I am unable to sit down, unable to eat and I cannot stop shaking. I can almost smell my own fear and, if I am like this now, what will I be like in four weeks' time?

Four days since I last updated my diary, only one of which was at all bearable. On visiting the doctor, I was persuaded to collect the medication he prescribed for me. Having done so, I can only wait and hope that I will indeed start to feel a bit better before too long. I continue to have feelings of real terror as the days go by and the trial approaches. I rarely leave the house as it is just too much effort. Plus I am becoming paranoid about seeing people. As recently as a month ago, I had no problems driving myself anywhere and everywhere but now the garden is the extent of my ventures. I feel as if my confidence is slowly ebbing away and the only time I am at ease with myself is when Ray is home from work.

I had an informal chat today with Steve the counsellor. Two hours passed quickly, with me doing all the talking while he just listened. I don't feel the need to see him on a regular basis, though. This one talk allowed me to clear my mind and that is what I needed to do. I have his number should the need arise to consult him again but there is no pressure on me to do so and that is good. The last thing I want is to be labelled as psychologically unstable!

September continues to be as hot as any summer day and there has been no rain. It is still a huge effort to do even the minimum of tasks and, on the occasions when I must leave the house, I feel very anxious. The weekend is slightly better because I have Ray for support.

We visit the cemetery and are approached by a father and son. During our conversation, it transpires that we know the family, albeit only slightly. They express their anger about what happened to Rachel and say that the whole community in which this deed occurred is furious too. That this hateful individual's address is within their territory makes them feel responsible for what happened there, despite everyone knowing that he had only recently moved into the area.

We are heartened when told by the younger man that Michael Little is having a hard time inside. The fact that this young man has just been released from the same penitentiary in which Little currently languishes makes his story most

Top: This was taken on the day of Rachel's baptism at our house in Ireland in April 1981. Rachel was three months old and is with, left to right, Kerry, John and Vanda (holding Rachel).

Bottom: Here she is aged one, with our cat, Poushka.

This was taken when she was aged about six months. I'm holding Rachel with her sister Vanda behind her and her brother John holding my hand.

This is the only picture of all six of us as a family, taken in 1986 or 1987. Ray and I are standing and seated are Vanda, Rachel, John and Kerry.

The day of her first Communion in the garden of our old house in June 1989. She was eight years old.

Top: Rachel aged 12 with our friend and priest, Father Michael White, on the day of her Confirmation in 1993.

Bottom: In the garden of our old house on the famous bike.

Aged 11, on the first day at St Mary's College, her senior school.

plausible. I make no excuses for feeling highly delighted that this coward may be getting a taste of his own medicine. For me, there is no such thing as innocent until proven guilty. We know, and he knows, what he did. The police know and so do many others. Whatever happens to him will not bring Rachel back, nor will it change anything. However, to have him live a long life of fear at the hands of his peers will bring some small solace to us and some vengeance for our precious girl.

It is less than three weeks now to the trial and we are becoming more fearful by the day. I feel physically sick and am unable to sleep. I am cold all the time and cannot stop shivering. Now that the time is drawing near, I just want it to happen now, not in three weeks. I want it over with, to face up to the horror and to try and start living again, in as good a way as I can.

I had a little visit yesterday from a lady from Victim Support, which passed an hour or so. We really only discussed court procedure and she offered to be with me up to me giving evidence. I don't really think I shall need her help but appreciate the offer regardless. Silly things are worrying me now, like where will we all park our cars during the trial? How long is it likely to last? I think that the less time it goes on for, the better for us, since that will mean the defence haven't much to fight with. But who knows with such things?

There are no more police visits so we are none the wiser as to how things are shaping up at this late stage. Mark's mother, Lorraine, is convinced that the plea will change to guilty on the day the trial starts, but the rest of us are unsure. Nothing will surprise me now. I am on edge and cannot wait for it to begin so that I may finally get some answers to my questions.

Hopefully I will feel better when the time comes and I have more of the family here for moral support.

Vanda is going to see the clairvoyant today. Nothing could have stopped her since Ray went. She admits to being nervous and I am too. I have to ask myself if we are all becoming mentally unstable, having to resort to this. I will not settle at all today until she has returned and spoken to me about her experience.

My stomach is seriously upset and I have the feelings of a cold coming on as well. I'll try to get through the day by being as busy as I can. I have a birthday cake to make for the weekend, which should keep my mind occupied, but in truth I have no heart for it. I still have not arranged the promised visit for my sister and niece. I don't know what they must think of me. I do want to see them but I just can't motivate myself, so it's much easier to keep putting them off.

A telephone call from Vanda's mobile. She is waiting to catch the bus home following her visit to the clairvoyant and seems a bit distressed. I can't stop shaking when she tells me some of what transpired during the consultation. Perhaps the most disturbing was the piece of paper she was given as she was leaving. On it was written, 'Night-night, Sis'. How could the woman have possibly known that this was how Rachel always signed herself off at the end of her text messaging to Vanda? I had certainly never heard of this before, so how could this stranger have made it up? It is all very odd, inexplicable and upsetting for us both. Vanda is shattered, tearful and only wants to be in her own home and left to her thoughts for the rest of the night.

I have got into the habit of going to bed very early these days. Sometimes I can hardly wait for 9pm to come around.

This is so unlike the me of old, who never retired before midnight, read for an hour or so and was still up early for work. However, it's many years since I slept through the night and this is compounded even more nowadays. I can drift off for a couple of hours but am awake and alert for much of the night and often up and dressed by 5.30am. Today is no exception.

I am downstairs by 6am and have a terrible feeling of fright today. I can't explain it but assume that it's the thought of the trial, only two and a half weeks away now. I tell Ray of this and he says that he, too, is terrified for the same reason. We both hope that Michael Little is experiencing at least some of the fears we feel.

The post arrives and with it is a reply to the letter I sent to little Rachel's mother in Ireland. It's a most beautiful letter with a lovely memorial bookmark of her Rachel. I am greatly heartened and touched by her words. She can identify with all that we are going through. She gives me her phone number and email address so that I can get in touch whenever I want to. I feel as if I have made a friend even though we have never met. I will certainly write back to her as soon as possible. I feel a little better now, a little less afraid and am convinced that this is my Rachel working on my behalf. It's her way of helping me to cope with whatever I have to face.

A call to Vanda brings me some quite disturbing news. Even though Mark has been told emphatically that he will not be called as a witness, it now seems the defence *will* be calling him. I am worried and not a little annoyed to hear of this. I am sure the police are working with the best of intentions but why do they never tell us these things? We seem to be kept in the dark about every little thing and it does nothing at all to boost our confidence. Another most worrying aspect is that they expect the trial to last for three weeks. This is a blow to me, because it must mean that the defence are going to make a real fight of it. We have been led to believe all along that the prosecution case is so strong that the defendant hasn't a hope. How then can it take as long as three weeks? I imagined that the evidence would be so damning that it would be all over in no more than one week. I am more worried than ever and wonder if I should telephone the police and ask for an explanation. I don't know what Ray's reaction will be to this latest piece of news, but it certainly won't be favourable.

A very bad and scary couple of days have passed, with my mind working in overdrive. I have had very little sleep and am up at the crack of dawn, wishing almost immediately that I was back in bed. So far, I have not allowed myself to take a nap during the day, even though it would be very easy to do so on many occasions.

I hear that Yorkshire Television want to do a tribute to Rachel, to be screened on the day of the verdict. I am to be asked to contribute to this. The reporter involved rings me today to confirm that this is indeed what they are intending to do. She seems rather surprised that the police have not been in touch with us regarding 13 October – what to expect, the protocols, etc. She seems more clued up than we are.

No sooner have I hung up the phone than a call comes through from our liaison officer. He tells me there is to be a conference tomorrow, when the Crown Prosecution Service, prosecution and defence will all meet to thrash out the final details. As a result of this meeting, he and his boss will visit us early next week. I am filled with trepidation and wonder exactly what they are coming for. What will they have to tell us? I ask if they expect any last-minute surprises from the defence and am told no and that I need have no worries. It is simply an administration exercise.

Somehow I cannot believe this. I am angry to think that our team will be sitting down with the enemy, so to speak, probably being civilised and even friendly. This is obviously the way these things work but it still seems wrong to me. At the end of the day, the defence are going to go all out to destroy Rachel's character whereas the prosecution are meant to be protecting it. How can that be right or fair?

When Ray comes home from work and is told of this, he is angry and upset. He has vowed to be here when the police arrive to speak to us, as has Vanda. I am highly relieved as I dread being here alone when they drop their bombshells. I have so many questions for them, none of which I'll remember when the time comes and I don't expect any answers in any case. I can only hope that I am reading more into this than I maybe should. Perhaps it really is merely protocol and I am letting my imagination run riot.

These final two weeks are definitely going to be the worst since Rachel's funeral and I wonder how we will get through them. It is going to be a very long and worrying weekend before the police arrive on Monday. The time now leading up to the trial will be the longest and hardest of my life.

The weekend is almost over, some bits bad and some slightly better than usual. I do feel easier when Ray and John are around but Sunday is still dismal. We try hard not to let our mood affect John, who is young and still has his life to lead. As the day wears on, we feel more morose and afraid. We aimlessly do a few necessary chores but are really only waiting for bedtime to come.

A small glimmer of light comes on Sunday evening when Father White drops in for an hour. It is easy to talk to him and he does realise what we are going through right now. We feel so alone and frightened. I hope that I can sleep for at least a few hours tonight, so that I am ready to face the police with a clear head tomorrow. I would describe our feelings at the moment as abject terror, since we do not know what they are likely to tell us when they turn up. We do suspect, however, that it will be nothing good.

Monday morning dawns and I don't want to sit around the house just waiting for the afternoon to come. I decide to drive out to the east of the city and do some shopping and browsing to take my mind off things. Again my stomach is upset but I am quite certain that it is just a case of nerves. I drive back and on the way stop at Vanda's to pick her up and bring her back for the meeting. I am quite early so we chat for a while before leaving. We are both nervous and imagine all sorts of silly things are about to unfold. Ray arrives home in good time to wash and tidy himself up before the appointed time of 2pm and John is home also.

In the event, only the police boss arrives as the liaison officer is otherwise engaged today. After some small talk and reassurances, we are given an update on the latest news. We are surprised to hear that the Friday meeting had also involved the judge, police and Michael Little. We are quite shocked by this – it was obviously not just an administration exercise at all. It was, effectively, a court hearing.

We are further surprised to learn that Little has not, in fact, changed his solicitor, as was previously suggested. He has had a change of barrister and this may be a problem for us. On Friday, his defence asked for more time in order to reexamine the case, at this late stage. Apparently, the judge denied this and said that the trial must start on 13 October as arranged. If it doesn't, there will no slot free until next year.

We are appalled to hear this and seriously worried. How will we cope if we have to live in this limbo indefinitely?

Again, we are assured by DS Paul Davison that there is an overwhelming case against Little and we need have no worries. It is easy to feel confident when he is with us in person and telling us this but will it all fall flat again once he has gone? I am sure that will be so, but, for the moment, we all feel better. Our only real concern now is that the trial will not go ahead on 13 October. We know it must open on that date but not whether it will be allowed to proceed, should his defence be unprepared. What a nightmare and certainly the last thing we were expecting to hear.

A worrying few days have passed, days spent updating the family about the uncertainty of the trial date. Ray's brother has already booked his flight from Ireland and Kerry time off work to be here. I am sure they'll both come anyway.

While I am out with Vanda on Thursday afternoon, Ray takes a call from our liaison officer. This is to say that I am to be called upon to give evidence on the first day of the trial, as will Mark.

I feel very unsettled and am scared when the phone rings later this night. It is another of our liaison officers who is still on duty and has been asked to call us with the very latest news. It seems that the trial will definitely go ahead, but now it will start on Tuesday, 14 October, 24 hours later than planned. I am still concerned and ask her repeatedly if it will really start on this day. She says that it has to, because the High Court judge has now decreed it. I wonder what has happened over the last couple of days to cause this. I don't know whether or not to believe this latest piece of information. After all that has occurred, we dare not relax in the slightest. We are told, however, to be at the Crown Court for 9.30am that day, for the trial to start at 10am. We can only hope and pray that it does indeed go ahead and all our waiting will finally come to an end.

We receive some more bad news over the weekend that may put a spanner in the works. Ray's brother, who is due to fly in from Ireland, may now not be able to make it. His wife's brother has had two massive heart attacks and is lying in a coma. He is only a young fellow, without a family of his own, so they must be there for him. It is very worrying at this late stage but we are all hoping that he pulls through.

Sadly, Pat dies at the weekend without regaining consciousness. Another blow for this family. He will be buried quite quickly, as is the norm over in Ireland, so Ray's brother will still be with us for the trial. I hope we feel better when we have a few family members round us, as we are all seriously afraid now.

Tuesday, 7 October 2003

The trial is due to start in exactly one week's time. It's hard to imagine that almost ten months have passed since we last saw Rachel. I still can't believe that she is never coming back again and keep wondering what she would make of all this notoriety. I hope I can keep myself together from now and until it is all over but it is becoming harder with every passing hour.

Friday, 10 October 2003

No time at all over the last three days to update my diary. A hectic time has ensued since I was last able to write anything at all and we have had a few more shocks since then.

My sister and niece visited us on Tuesday and stayed for a couple of hours. Our spirits were lifted somewhat as they kept us highly entertained. Father White also appeared for a time while they were here and seemed almost mesmerised by their bizarre behaviour! No sooner had they all left than we had a further two visitors, so it was rather later than usual when we finally got to bed. Despite this, I was still awake and up for most of the night. Nothing new there, then!

Wednesday morning found us as low as ever and very fearful once more. It was a free day for Ray and me but we did nothing in particular to pass the time apart from visiting the cemetery as usual. We are still keeping the flowers as nice as we can on a daily basis and will continue to do so when Rachel's headstone is in place. It won't be too long now.

There's a call this evening from Ray's sister Maureen in Ireland and, on this occasion, I speak to her first. It seems that Pat's funeral went as well as one could hope and we discuss this and that in general. I then say that I wonder who the third person in this family will be the next to go and am shocked when Maureen says she has some bad news for us. I immediately think of Ray's youngest sister whose husband, we know, has been unwell for some months. This young man does indeed have some serious problems, but it is not him. Ray's brother-in-law in America is in a very bad way, at death's door we are told, and this is certainly a great shock. He has developed an infection throughout his entire body following minor surgery and also been diagnosed with diabetes. We are dreadfully sorry to hear this and think back to happy holidays in Ireland with him and his wife over the years, as well as their visits to us in England.

We ring his office in Chicago at once and are heartened to hear that he has had his best night so far. His wife, Ray's sister Jean, is with him, along with their four children and we can only pray that he pulls through. What more can possibly befall this family in the year of 2003?

Another very uneasy night follows this news, and neither of us gets much sleep. We know that tomorrow we are due more visitors and, in truth, we find it very wearying.

On Thursday morning, my aunt and her daughter arrive. Ray is out taking Vanda to a hospital appointment. I receive a phone call from one of our liaison officers and immediately get the jitters. I am shocked rigid when he casually tells me that the first witness to be called on the first day of the trial will be our son, John. This is the very first time that he has been mentioned and I don't know what to think at this late stage. I am to be the second witness on the first day. The officer wanted to call round during the afternoon for a more in-depth discussion but I explain that I am expecting the TV reporter at 1.30pm and will be taping an interview for the tribute to Rachel. We arrange that two officers will now call on Monday, 13 October instead.

All manner of worries and fears are running through my mind now and I wish only that my aunt and cousin would leave so I can think things through. To sit and analyse the situation, to try and imagine why, at this late stage, they have decided to call upon John's testimony at the trial.

I get little respite, however, since no sooner has this call ended than I receive yet another, this time from a different liaison officer. I am unsure what to make of it since, on the face of it, it is merely a courtesy call. Or is it? After some formalities, the subject turns to current media interest in the trial. I feel I am being given the gypsy's warning — do not speak to any of them before or during the trial. This warning is unnecessary since we have kept our cards close to our chests so far and we are not about to change that now. It seems there has been press interest in showing pictures of Michael Little's flat (the crime scene) but I am told that this will only happen with our approval. We need to discuss this as a family, along with Mark. I think it is a very sensitive issue but at this moment I personally have no objection to it.

Apparently, there is also a police video of the scene which, I am told, we can view, should we wish to do so. I am unsure about this. I don't know if I could bring myself to look at this but maybe Vanda would wish to see it.

I am perturbed by both of these calls and know that Ray will not take the news of John's summons well. When he returns, he sees at once that I am very uneasy and I tell him what has transpired during his absence. He is furiously angry and rages at everyone and everything, including me. He shoots me down as the messenger, but I am expecting it and so am not unduly upset. He calms himself down eventually but I am most concerned as to what he will be like come Monday when the police turn up. I imagine that he will let his feelings be known in no uncertain terms and, sadly, I cannot chicken out of that meeting. If only I could ...

There is no time for any real discussion, however, as the Yorkshire Television reporter is due imminently so we must put on a front for her. I had been expecting just the one girl, Tina Gelder, to arrive for an informal chat and am therefore dismayed to see she is accompanied by a cameraman. I had imagined that, at the most, we would talk into a tape recorder about Rachel but the intention is for Ray and I to do an actual interview on camera. It seems pointless and churlish to demur but, had I known of this earlier, I could have made more of an effort with my appearance!

It is very easy to talk to Tina. She is not at all intrusive and doesn't once mention the forthcoming court case. It is just our own thoughts and memories of Rachel that she is interested in. Ray speaks most eloquently, although, on this occasion, I don't really have much to say. Later we go outside and are filmed near the rose garden and next to the place that I created for Rachel. It is a very poignant moment but we try not to let it upset us.

Although I am still terribly afraid that, by some quirk of fate, Michael Little walks free, I can't imagine they would be planning to show this tribute to Rachel afterwards should there be the remotest possibility of that happening. Still, that worry is at the back of my mind and everyone else's, I am sure.

John gets up after his night shift and prepares for work again tonight. He has to be told that he is being called as the first witness now. As I had suspected, the news does not go down well and it is hard to know if he is angry or simply afraid. Like me, he wonders why he wasn't called from the beginning, but who knows? It could mean nothing at all, yet we can only see the negative side of things. Could there be an ulterior motive in the prosecution's need of John at this late stage? How long have they known they would be calling him and does it mean that things are not progressing in quite the way they have led us to believe? No doubt we will find out more on Monday but, until then, our confidence is diminished even further. We are more afraid, more on edge than ever and are rapidly losing the plot.

I find that I can't eat a thing and my nerves are so shattered that I do the unthinkable – I have a stiff drink quite early in the evening, even though I am expecting my brother Paul to arrive at any time. He is taking me to his house as I am due to have my hair done there tonight. Meanwhile, Father White arrives and, while Ray is upstairs, I give him a brief update on today's developments. I know that he is worried and upset for us and notice, too, that he looks very tired. This whole thing is getting to him in the same way that it is getting to us all. He also has the added worry of a very ill housekeeper.

My brother arrives and I leave Ray and Father White alone together. I can have a couple of hours' respite with my family while I have my hair done. It's hard tonight though. Conversation is somewhat stilted and I want only to get back home quickly. Even my hair doesn't turn out as well as it normally does so I must be truly out of sorts with myself. Everyone, I know, is rooting for us and wishing us all the luck in the world for next week. I am sure I won't see many people now before the trial begins but promise to ring and update everyone as it progresses from day to day.

Ray is waiting up for me. He has spoken to Ronnie, his brother in Ireland, who has told Ray that his flight leaves Dublin at 8.30pm on Sunday, 12 October. We will drive to Leeds airport to collect him. Kerry plans to leave Southampton on Monday morning to drive up here and she should arrive sometime during the afternoon. She will be staying with us as she wishes to sleep in Rachel's old room at the family home, so we also have to arrange for Ronnie to stay at a local hotel for the duration. This suits him well though, as he would rather have his own company a lot of the time. I so much want them both to arrive. I need their support and common sense, as two who are on the periphery of this nightmare rather than in the middle as we, the rest of the family, have been for months.

The only good thing at the moment is that we are finally pulling together and drawing some comfort from each other. Such a relief and a difference from the way things were a few short weeks ago and I thank God for it. We have to remain strong for this final push. This is the last thing we can do for Rachel. We owe it to her and we cannot and will not let her down. If she is somewhere looking down on us, I hope she is proud of what we are trying to do for her. Above all, I pray that she gets the justice she deserves in the end. Not because of what happened to Rachel do I advocate the return of the death penalty. I have always held that view but perhaps the deterrent would have prevented the likes of Michael Little doing what he did to her. As it is, I can think of no sentence that would compare with his crime, which is why I say 'justice — *for what it's worth*'.

The weekend looms ahead, the last before the start of the trial, please God. There is much to do in readiness for our guests but I am strangely reluctant to make a start. Somehow, changing the bed linen and other such mundane chores seem unimportant in the greater scheme of things but I suppose they must be done.

I can't imagine that I will find much time to update my diary between now and the trial, which is only three days away. I will make great efforts though after the final visit from the police on Monday afternoon to record all that transpires on that occasion. I dare not even think about Tuesday morning. The very idea of it fills me with dread and I don't want to consider how we are all going to get through the next week or so, or however long the trial may last. Having to hear, in terrible detail, what happened to Rachel, and to see the face of her killer during it, does not bear thinking about. I must stay strong for everybody but wonder how we are all going to be able to live with the cold, hard facts for the rest of our lives.

These final few days are definitely the most nerve-wracking of all so far and, if ever I was in need of prayer, then surely I am now.

Saturday, 11 October 2003

Just when we thought things could get no worse, we get up to discover that the back window of one of our cars has been smashed to pieces. We didn't hear a thing during the night so we have no idea of what time this latest upset occurred. The fact that the car was way up the drive behind closed gates leads us to believe that something was thrown at the window with force, maybe from a distance. Nothing has been taken and, in fact, this car is only our run-around, not one of our two better ones. Thankfully, they are in our garage.

Ray at once arranges for a replacement window to be fitted today – yet more expense that we can ill afford, not to mention the inconvenience. I feel so sorry for Ray as he has to drive miles out of the city to have the job done. He feels very disheartened and who could blame him? I shall have to try extra hard to lift his spirits over the weekend. The plans we had made for today will have to be put on the back burner for the time being but at least Ray's brother Ronnie arrives tomorrow and hopefully that will help us all. On balance, a shattered window counts for nothing but it is just one further blow to a family who thought they had endured it all this year.

At least the weather is holding up and it is still glorious for mid-October. It is still possible to hang out a line of washing and know that by the end of the day it will have dried, and the garden is still looking pretty good. Small consolation.

I feel like doing nothing at all today but must rouse myself. I cannot let myself sink into despair at this stage. There are things that should be done this weekend as, once the trial begins, none of us will have the time, energy or inclination to do everyday tasks. By no means is the house in the pristine order that it once was, nor have I kept on top of the ironing etc. I have, however, done some baking for the freezer, in the event that our guests might want to eat. I certainly can't see myself cooking meals after we have been in court all day, but I am sure we won't starve!

On Sunday, Ray and I have a little respite as we drive to Leeds airport to collect his brother Ronnie, who is flying in from Dublin. We are really looking forward to seeing him again. There are a few minor hiccups en route to the airport as we try to find the easiest way, but we arrive in good time, just as the plane is arriving. We are waiting to greet Ronnie as he emerges from the terminal and his giant presence gives me some comfort. I am sure Ray feels this way too and we are all quite emotional.

Monday, 13 October 2003

I try to put the house in some sort of order but, in truth, it doesn't take much effort. We three, Ray, John and I, have made very little mess over the past months, with the kitchen barely being used.

I iron copious amounts of shirts for the two men, who intend to dress formally each day of the trial. They will get through an awful lot of shirts if the trial lasts up to three weeks! There is food for Kerry, should she wish to eat when she arrives tonight. All that remains now is for me to lay out my own outfit for tomorrow, take a bath and try to sort out my hair, which is becoming more unruly with every day that passes!

There's a brief visit from the police and Ronnie is with us at the time. More reassurances that the evidence is so overwhelming that it cannot but go well. Are we convinced? No, but we must put our trust in these people. Afterwards, I realise that we have asked them nothing at all, so scared are we of tomorrow's ordeal.

Kerry is with us in the evening, very tired following her 260-mile drive. She too has had to cook, bake and freeze for her family, so they can survive while she is away. Initially, she will be here for one week and after that we shall have to see what can be arranged. Nobody has a lot to say tonight and we are all in bed at a reasonable hour. Tomorrow is going to be a tough, tough day.

Tuesday, 14 October 2003
– Day One

The first day of the trial – it has finally begun. We are up early because Ray and I wish to visit Rachel before we leave for court. We have to tell her that it is the day we have long been awaiting, albeit with dread – the start of our fight for justice for our daughter.

On our arrival at the cemetery, which is empty at this early hour, we are amazed to see a beautiful jet-black cat – the same one that was near by soon after we first laid Rachel to rest – as we approach her grave. We took it on that occasion as a sign from her and feel even more so now that she is truly still with us. The cat is completely unafraid of our presence and spends some time ignoring us, stepping daintily between the flowers adorning her plot. It rubs against the photographs of Rachel there, before walking off and disappearing. It is quite eerie, although we feel strangely comforted as we leave for home.

Our intention is to arrive at the court at around 9.30am but we must first collect Ronnie before going on to get Vanda and her friend Margaret, who will be with us throughout the whole trial. We do this and all admit to feeling very nervous, not knowing what awaits us. Luckily, Kerry has just got a new car, a people-carrier which seats seven comfortably, so we are all able to travel together. We feel there is safety in numbers and cling to each other for support. We expect that quite a few of our and Rachel's friends will be waiting for us, including her very best friend, Saoirse, who is taking time off from her job in Surrey to be here. Her old school friend Adam, who was so devastated at the funeral, has also promised his support. We are so grateful to all concerned and, sure enough, true to their word, everyone is there for us already.

The media is out in force, awaiting our arrival, as we expected. Some of them we have got to know quite well over the past months and they seem almost like old friends now, so we are happy to greet them. Others among them are strangers to us, sent, I suspect, by the national press. There is discomfort at their presence and the flashing of the cameras is very disconcerting but we shall have to get used to it. They, as well as we, are here for the long haul.

For John, Mark and myself, today will be frustrating. We know that, as witnesses for the prosecution, we cannot go into the courtroom until we have given our evidence. We must miss the swearing-in of the jury and the opening speeches. We have also been warned not to question anyone afterwards about the content of their evidence. They in turn should not give us any information either. We are to remain in ignorance for the time being. Feeling cheated, we watch everyone else file into court.

As it happens, everybody leaves the courtroom very soon afterwards. Due to legal wrangling, the court is adjourned almost as soon as it begins. The prosecution have made their opening speech but the defence team have asked for an adjournment. They argue that, because they have only recently inherited Michael Little as a client, they have not had sufficient time to prepare their case. If they have their way, the trial will be stopped and put back to a later date. This is the one thing we had been afraid of and the thought of having to wait many more months for a new date to be set does not bear contemplating.

Thankfully, the judge is not swayed by this argument and merely gives the defence the remainder of this day to get their act together. Common sense has prevailed. It has been a mostly wasted day but we are assured that the trial will definitely get under way tomorrow and we are much relieved. We have crossed the first hurdle, but how many more have we to face?

We stop to buy the local paper on the way home. They have wasted no time in reporting today's events. It is impossible for my eye to miss. A full front-page picture of Rachel under the headline: RACHEL MURDER: ACCUSED — I MUST BE EVIL.' It is quite a shock to see that but it will have no bearing on the evidence that I shall be giving.

None of the family speaks to me about today's proceedings and I do not ask, although I do read the report i.1 the paper. After all, it has not been said that I shouldn't. It looks like most of the prosecution's opening speech is printed here, none of which seems as if it has any relevance to what my own evidence will be, nor John's or Mark's, for that matter. It is all about Michael Little's arrest and confession, most of which I know already. It is clear that Mr Marson, our barrister, has spoken about Rachel, outlining her background, medical history and her relationship with Mark — no secrets there for me either.

I see that Little's words at the crime scene have been mentioned and how his arrest came about. Again, nothing confidential in that; I had already been given a brief resume of all of this beforehand. Rather worrying is the fact that, even though we know of his original confession and are glad that it is being allowed in evidence against him, we are aware that he has since changed his story, not once, but twice. This is all we know so far, but that too may change after today's briefing with his team. There could yet be a final version of his story, one that the police and CPS are not aware of at this stage. It must be dreadfully worrying for them, not to mention frustrating.

Meanwhile, we must wait until tomorrow to see what transpires. I am quaking at the prospect of giving evidence and I am sure that John and Mark are equally as fearful. It's good to think, though, that Little's days of hiding away from the truth are numbered. Before very much longer, we — and the public at large — will be enlightened. Let us hope that his original confession will be enough to condemn him.

Despite not being in court today to hear for myself what was said, I find reading the report in the paper soul-destroying. I feel so very drained and weary, and today is only the start, the tip of the iceberg. How, I wonder, can we possibly endure what surely must ensue? Tomorrow is another day and one that I am dreading. I only hope that I can fulfil all that is required of me when I take the stand and I pray above all that I can face up to the defence barrister. I know that I must, for Rachel's sake. Let battle commence ...

Wednesday, 15 October 2003
– Day Two

Ronnie has decided to make his own way to the court today so this morning we have only to pick up Vanda and Margaret. It has been a sleepless night for me, and it is an early start for us all again. Ray goes to the cemetery at 8am as he intends to do each morning. I will not go on a daily basis. I do not feel the need because I know that Rachel will be with me in spirit throughout the long days that lie ahead. I cling to this thought and try to draw comfort from it.

This morning will start where yesterday left off. The defence will give their opening speech and then it is the turn of John, Mark and myself to give our evidence. We are taken into an anteroom and given our original statements to read through. Just prior to this, one of our liaison officers takes me aside and has a private word. It is about my sighting of Little as he walked past our home early on New Year's morning while I was standing outside in conversation with Rachel. I am asked if I have told anyone of this occurrence and I can truly say that, with the exception of a few immediate family members, nobody knows about it. Even Mark and his mother are not aware of it. Although my word is not doubted, it seems this incident will not be brought up by our barrister, Mr Marson, during my questioning. I do wonder why but don't press the issue, although it seems rather crucial. It seems that it doesn't really matter too much as far as tangible evidence is concerned because they have more than enough of that already.

Back in the anteroom, I am now so nervous that I can barely read through my statement. John and Mark are similarly affected. We each find an odd sentence or phrase that requires amending and are assured that it will be done. It all seems so long ago now that none of us can clearly remember what we said at the time.

The most horrifying aspect of it all for me is that it seems there has been a change of plan since yesterday. I am now to be the first witness called, not John as we were originally told. I am glad that I wasn't told this until now, as it means I have less time to dwell on it and what it could mean.

I am given a few words of encouragement from the Witness Support volunteer who offers to accompany me into the court, which he does and then sits behind me on the stand. I have been advised to keep my answers to the bare minimum and not to deviate or add anything unnecessarily. I think this is sound advice as, if I adhere to this, there is less chance of my being challenged by the defence. I suppose it helps that I am a calm person anyway and rarely open my mouth without thinking first. Taking the oath is very nerve-racking and I stumble over some of the words. Luckily, I quickly regain my composure. Mr Marson puts me at ease more or less immediately. In reality, it is not such an ordeal, nothing like I expected it to be.

I am quizzed about Rachel, her relationship with us, her family, with Mark, and also about her younger years. Mr Marson mentions her love of dancing and her happy-go-lucky nature. I realise these questions are just to try and ease me into it. He now moves on to the night in question and there are a few awkward moments for me when Rachel's demeanour is queried. I am forced to admit that she was angry to discover that Mark was not at home, that she was upset and carried on in a way that I had never known before. I feel so disloyal to Mark when I make this admission, but I have sworn to tell the truth and that is how it was. She was annoyed, upset and overwrought; her attitude had really shocked me at the time.

My telephone calls to Rachel are discussed in detail and the fact that she didn't answer any of them. Mr Marson seems to make an issue of this and also asks me what Rachel had on her person when she left me. I tell him that, apart from her handbag, she had a £10 note in her jacket pocket, along with her cigarettes and lighter. These items were never recovered which is why, I imagine, he put such emphasis on them. Somebody had spent that money and smoked her cigarettes but it certainly wasn't her.

A very difficult part follows when, at a signal from Mr Marson, the exhibits officer brings forward a fairly large wooden case with a glass front. Inside is the dress Rachel was wearing that night, along with her jacket. I must detach myself – it is the only way. The dress is not so bad as, being claret-coloured, not a lot shows up, but the jacket is a different matter altogether. It is covered with white paper arrows pointing in every direction, which signify the angle at which the knife entered her body. I thank the Lord that this box is not clearly visible from the public gallery as the sight of its contents would devastate Ray and the others. No parent should ever have to identify such an item as belonging to their own child. How very, very sad that her delight in the new garment would be so short-lived. She only got to wear it for a few hours in the end.

Next on the agenda is the screening of the CCTV footage that captured Rachel soon after she left me to walk home. Mr Marson asks if I can identify the person shown as being her 'without a shadow of a doubt'. Yes. How very vulnerable she looks and how forlorn. Head down and arms crossed over her chest as she is walking away from me for the very last time. If only I knew then what I know now …

Mr Marson's questioning is over and I have weathered it well enough so far, I think. I haven't faced the defence yet and I have noticed their barrister, Mr Kadri, has been watching me intently throughout my evidence. He looks ready to pounce but, to my surprise, when the judge asks him, he replies, 'No questions, your honour.' I have been let off the hook and it is such a big relief, even though I had prepared myself for a grilling. I don't know how I would have reacted to the defence and now, thankfully, I never will. Perhaps Mr Kadri, in his wisdom, realised it would be a bad move to try and intimidate the mother of the victim.

I feel quite shaken as I stand down and leave the room. I do not look towards the public gallery. I only hope that I haven't disappointed the family or let Rachel down in any way. I did my very best and that is all I can say about it.

John is the next witness and I am back in the anteroom calming myself down when he enters the court. I don't think I could face being in there while my son gives evidence since I know how upset and nervous he is. Maybe once he has said his piece we can meet up and go back in to listen to Mark's testimony.

Perhaps 20 or 30 minutes pass before John re-emerges on to the concourse and he is highly agitated, to say the least. He did not escape a cross-examination and he isn't best pleased. In fact, he is very angry. It seems Mr Kadri suggested to John that, although he described Rachel's relationship with Mark as 'comfortable and happy', she could still have been 'open to offers'! I can well imagine that John would see red at this scurrilous inference but I know, too, that he is well able to fight his corner. He is eloquent and articulate and through his work has spoken in public on many occasions. I cannot imagine that he was easily intimidated and at 6ft 5in he is a very imposing figure to boot.

Both he and I are upset now, John because he didn't realise how his words would be twisted and me because I don't like to think that my son's integrity has been questioned. Neither of us wishes to be in the courtroom while Mark is on the stand. After the way John has been cross-examined, what hope does Mark have? He is already so nervous, so distraught and not at all as able as John to defend himself. I am very fearful, and not, it seems, without just cause.

Sometime later, Mark comes storming out in floods of tears, though whether they are tears of sorrow or rage I cannot tell. He is followed closely by Ray, who is looking concerned and puts an arm around Mark to comfort him. He tells him what a great job he did on the stand. Whatever has happened in there was obviously very nasty as Mark is extremely rattled.

Apparently, the defence made similar suggestions to Mark as had been made to John, regarding Rachel's allegiance to Mark. That, along with other little barbs to try to imply that their relationship was on the skids, at rock bottom. Mr Kadri made a big issue of the fact that they had spent Christmas at their respective family homes, rather than with each other. So what? That is what they did every year, preferring to exchange their gifts to each other on Boxing Day and making a big deal out of that day instead. To us and to them, there was nothing unusual in this. It certainly didn't mean that Rachel would have been on the lookout for someone like Michael Little on her way home at New Year!

Poor Mark. It is obvious that he has been through the mill and we have had a taste of what is sure to come. We can guess at the tactics that the defence will be using in order to exonerate their client. We three, along with Ray, go back into court and are in time to hear much of the evidence of the next witness.

This turns out to be a young man called Nathan Tempest, who at one time had been a good enough friend of Little to share a flat with him. He also spent part of the evening of New Year's Eve with Little in a local bar, just yards from our own home.

I am unsure what to make of this young man who, naturally enough, is said to have disowned Little entirely. He seems quite excitable but rather too sure of himself while on the stand. I get the impression he is relishing his moment of fame.

His evidence is that Little was 'in a mood' for much of the evening and, as the night wore on, he became even more agitated. This, he says, was because he left Little to go off and play the slot machines and because a girl whom Little liked the look of ignored him, choosing instead to talk to him, Nathan Tempest. This had caused some unpleasantness as Little then started mouthing obscenities at the girl.

Tempest goes on to say that he, himself, was going to a party to which he had been invited and when he left the pub Little was still there, talking to another acquaintance of theirs. That was the last he had seen of Little that night. The next day, he and another friend had gone around to Little's flat but, to his surprise, he had been left on the doorstep. Every other time he had been there, Little had invited him in but, this time, he had had to ask to be let in. Little seemed reluctant but finally admitted him.

Tempest then describes the conditions in which this beast lived – in filth and squalor, existing on takeaways and junk food and rarely bathing. This is the place where my beautiful, fastidious girl ended her days – nothing more than a stinking hovel. I cannot bear to think of this, never mind her final few moments there.

As I have expected, Nathan Tempest is cross-examined in minute detail by Mr Kadri, who makes a meal of him. This young man is no match for a hard-nosed professional who is well used to tearing people's testimony to shreds. Tempest does his level best and in no way disgraces himself, but the defence have done their homework and can no doubt see how easy it will be to tie him in knots. A particularly bad exchange ensues when Little's clothing is called into question. The shirt that Tempest says Little was wearing that night is disputed by the defence. It is a real bone of contention and there are a few heavy moments during that argument.

The CCTV footage is now shown to Tempest for the first time. It is also perfectly visible to the rest of the court. The man shown is identified immediately as Michael Little. Tempest is quite certain that it is him (as is everyone else in the room). Mr Kadri ridicules his certainty, nit-picking on every point of recognition and wanting to know, in fine detail, how Tempest comes to the conclusion that it is indeed Little. He is wanting, I imagine, to coerce Tempest into doubting himself but it is a forlorn hope. This young man will not be budged. He knows for sure that he is not mistaken. It *is* Little.

I can hardly take my eyes off the haunting image of Little rolling along the screen, cigarette in hand. It only confirms my own certainty that it was indeed him who had walked ahead of Rachel as she left me that morning. Apart from the clothing, shape and size, he has such a unique gait that it can be nobody but him.

It is the first time we see Little show any sign of animation, as he cranes his neck to see himself on the screen. I wonder how he feels now. The camera never lies, even though he may try to do so over the coming days.

A break for lunch and a trip to fortify ourselves at the nearest hostelry. I feel I will need as much Dutch courage as possible to see me through what is to come. No doubt lists have been drawn as to the sequence of the witnesses but we are not aware of them beforehand. We don't know who, or what, to expect this afternoon.

The first person to appear is a young man of whom we had no prior knowledge. He turns out to be a mutual acquaintance of Little and Tempest who was with them in the pub on New Year's Eve. He seems a decent enough lad. He had, from what transpires, taken pity on Little after Tempest had left that night and, seeing him alone, had invited him along to a family party at the home of his aunt, whom he had first telephoned for permission.

The house is about two miles away from the pub – easily within walking distance. The young man says that he really didn't know Little well at all but, despite that, was happy enough to take him to his aunt's house. At the party, Little was quiet and did not really socialise with the other guests, though he did have quite a few drinks. He stated at one point that he should not be drinking at all, due to the medication he was taking.

Shortly after midnight, Little said that he was going home and was escorted to the front door, where he took his leave. There were some concerns about him walking home alone at that hour and he was asked to telephone them on reaching home to let them know he had arrived safely. The young chap waited in vain for Little's call – it never came. We are told it was some days later that the lad caught up with Little and the question of his journey home was raised. Little allegedly reported that he had got home OK and had simply forgotten to call.

The next witness on the stand is the aunt whose party Little attended. When asked to describe Little, his clothing etc. I am given an immediate little thrill – her recollection of him that night tallies perfectly with my own! The colour of his shirt, the fact that he appeared to be clean shaven and with very short hair. This is exactly how he looked to me as he walked by that night even though, by all accounts, he didn't look at all like this at the time of his arrest. When he appeared in court for the first time, on 31 January, he had a goatee beard and average-length hair, but of course he'd had a whole month in which to grow both. I feel justified in the knowledge that I was right in my critical assessment of Little. I was beginning to doubt myself and, for sure, those of the family who were aware of my insistence that I *had* seen him were sceptical.

As her nephew before her, this lady asserts that the time of Little's departure was no later than 12.45am and does not falter under cross-examination. I see no reason for either of them to lie under oath, especially as they have no axe to grind. They are not acquainted with us or Rachel.

It all seems to be falling into place now, even the timing is right. Given the distance involved between the aunt's house and our own, Little should have definitely been passing by Rachel and I at the time in question, that being the route he took.

My poor, poor girl. Had she continued on her way the first time she left, she would have been way ahead of him. Why, oh why did she come back inside? To smoke another cigarette and change her shoes? It is so hard to accept that fate could be so cruel.

Witnesses are coming thick and fast this afternoon and are being processed without delay. We are aware of the next one, though not in any great detail. The witness is a taxi driver, but I have no idea of what his evidence will be.

He gives an account of his movements on New Year's Eve, obviously a busy night for his profession. He tells the court that, on the way to pick up a fare that morning, he saw a girl matching Rachel's description, halfway between our house and her own. I am sure he took little notice of her then, but he does remember that she was speaking to a man with a dog at the time. She seemed to be smiling and walking away in the opposite direction, unconcerned and on her own. This sounds like Rachel – she would happily pass the time of day with anyone and she particularly loved animals, so she had probably stopped to pet this one.

A short time later, having picked up his fare, the taxi driver saw the same girl but this time, she was much closer to where Rachel would have turned off for home. He estimated the time to be around 2.15am. She was still alone and seemed as unconcerned as before. That was the last he saw of her but, having recognised the description put out by the media, he immediately contacted the police. Thank God for such people. At least we are able to build up a picture of Rachel's last movements.

One more witness follows, another one of whom we are unaware – a young man who was driving along the road that Rachel took that night, together with his wife. The man describes seeing a tall, slim, blonde-haired girl walking in the opposite direction to the one they were going. There was nothing untoward about her and she was alone. There was no sign of the man with the dog. This man recognised the girl as being Rachel after seeing her picture in the papers and on the television, and so contacted the police.

I do not doubt in either case that it was her, for how many girls can have been out that night, in that place, at that time, fitting her description? The fact that she was alone and seemingly unafraid speaks volumes in itself. The evidence of these two men points to the obvious conclusion that Rachel had no qualms about walking the short distance home on her own. She was unafraid and saw no danger. Had she done so, she would not have set off in the first place. Michael Little's lies to the contrary are just that – lies. But more of that later.

The afternoon continues and there is at least one more

witness who will give evidence, one who is known to us this time. We hadn't known until now at what point he would be called to the stand. This detective constable was, in fact, the first policeman who came to see us after we reported Rachel's disappearance. He is here today in a different capacity, however. His responsibility during the inquiry has been to sift through the CCTV footage, a subject he has become rather expert on, by all accounts.

In the very early days, the film from the supermarket's camera, which is less than five minutes from our house, had been requested and he was able to isolate certain figures. The first of these has already been seen by the court and identified by Nathan Tempest as being Michael Little. The date on the film was 1-1-03 and the time 1.59am. The second figure, taken from the same film, is timed at 2.01am and I have already identified it as being Rachel. How close behind him she was at that point, and how unconcerned. Undoubtedly, she was not even aware of him ahead of her. The footage is very clear and there can be no mistake at all that we are, indeed, seeing Rachel and Little.

Not so clear is what follows in the next sequences. As well as some taken from private houses in the vicinity, some footage has been acquired from a local school, which is within sight of both Little's and Rachel's flats. There are images on this film, the timing of which tallies with the evidence of both of the witnesses who say they saw Rachel. The taxi driver puts the time he saw her at around 2.15am, at the spot where she would have cut across from the main road to go round the school perimeter to reach home. The school's camera, it would seem, verifies that this is what occurred, for it is timed only minutes later.

I am able to make out a female figure as it comes into view and it certainly looks like Rachel, although this image is nowhere near as clear as the supermarket footage. It is noticeable that it is a tall person, wearing a dark top with a slightly lighter skirt. Very fair hair can be seen as well as what are most definitely a pair of pale legs ending in white shoes. I can't think that there would be too many people abroad that morning fitting this description. Even less likely is that another girl's movements could so identically match Rachel's at the relevant time. I do not believe in those kinds of coincidences.

I feel very afraid while viewing this. I can't explain why, only that it is like watching a spine-chilling movie and knowing what is about to happen. The film is something that we knew existed but we had no idea of its content until this moment.

The footage plays on in a slightly jerky fashion and now we see another figure come into view. It is quite grainy and not too clear an image, but it is obviously that of a male. The person in question is following the female and is only a few steps behind her, less than 40 seconds away.

This is very ominous and quite breathtaking. An eerie silence prevails throughout the courtroom as everyone tries to digest what they are seeing. In the absence of any other person on the tape, the timing and the close proximity to Little's home, one can only conclude that the two figures must be those of Little and Rachel. What other logical explanation could there be? It will be difficult, though, to prove any of this and being certain in one's own mind is not enough. The jury will have to decide what they think of this admittedly rather flimsy piece of evidence.

I am just horrified now, to think that Little might have deliberately hung back at this point, to let Rachel overtake him. Did he, I wonder, always intend to accost her before she reached home? If not by fair means, by foul?

Thursday, 16 October 2003
– Day Three

Today we are to hear the evidence of the police officers who had the unenviable task of searching Little's flat, one of whom actually discovered Rachel's body hidden there. We are only told of their scheduled appearance on reaching court this morning but it comes as no huge surprise. We have been expecting these three witnesses to be brought into the proceedings quite early on.

We await the first witness's arrival with trepidation. Soon we will hear, in his own words, exactly what happened and what Little said at the time of his arrest. It is hard to imagine whether this knowledge will make us feel better or worse, when we have spent so very long tormenting ourselves with every scenario we could think of.

He is a very young, fresh-faced constable who was still only a probationer at the time. What a baptism of fire for him. I sense that he is very nervous but I have great faith in his capabilities, knowing that the police team had been highly impressed with the professional way in which he had handled things then.

As the story unfolds, we learn that he was one of a team of three who were sent out to do house searches on the morning of 28 January. It was a filthy day, raining, windy and bitterly cold. It was four weeks to the day since Rachel had disappeared and it can't have been a pleasant prospect to have to go knocking on doors unannounced.

Little opens the door to the flat after the second knock and they state their business. He shows no emotion as he allows them inside, where nothing untoward is noticed. In the flat is a friend of Little, whom he has known since his early school days. The friend is on the point of leaving when the police arrive but is prevented from doing so while the search is in progress.

As the police are leaving, they ask what is behind the door on the landing outside the flat. Years ago these cupboards were used as coal sheds, but nowadays they are generally utilised for storage. Little says that he uses it for rubbish, to which his friend laughs and says, 'And I bet it stinks in there!' Little is asked to unlock it, to which he replies that he has no key. This does not satisfy the constables and, after further delaying tactics, Little produces a set of keys and makes an attempt to find one that will fit. He eventually selects a key but pretends that it will not open the door. It is an act, as the policeman says he obviously is turning the key in the wrong direction.

One of the officers takes over and Little stands back. At this point, the friend is standing in the doorway of the flat and watching the proceedings. The cupboard is about 3ft high and crammed to the ceiling with cardboard boxes and old pieces of carpet. A terrible smell pervades, likened to rotting meat.

A second officer begins to move the rubbish aside and sees what he takes to be a mannequin or tailor's dummy, pushed into the back. On touching what he thinks is the foot, he is horrified to realise that it is soft and human, a fact that shocks him to the core.

In disbelief, he goes into the flat to fetch his colleague to confirm that what he has found is, indeed, a human body. The probationer is left inside with Little who says at once, 'It's her. I need to get it off my chest. I have wanted to tell someone, or someone to find her for so long.' He goes on to say that he hasn't told anyone else and has kept the secret to himself. That he couldn't be normal, he must be evil because a normal person would not do that. He wanted to see a counsellor or someone.

I believe every word of that statement.

By now, all three officers are fully aware of the grim discovery they have stumbled upon. It is Rachel. I am sure that none of them expected such an outcome when they set out that morning. I feel so sorry for them, more so for the one who first realised it was her. The shock must have been so severe.

While one of them stays guard outside the cupboard, another calls for reinforcements. There are 100 officers within a one-mile radius this day, all involved in the house searches. The probationer is left with Little and the friend inside the flat. It cannot have been easy for him, being as inexperienced as he was. He states that the friend is almost demented, pacing around and shouting at Little, 'Do you know anything about this?' to which he replies, 'Yeah.' This friend desperately wants to leave Little and the flat but is made to stay where he is. He sinks into a chair and sits rocking backwards and forwards, seemingly in deep shock.

Little starts to talk, alleging what happened that night, and he will not be silenced, even though the young copper warns him not to say anything. When it becomes clear that Little is determined to speak, the probationer writes everything down, which is a confession of his guilt.

He says that he had been on the street that night as Rachel was walking past – presumably meaning the time when they were within yards of each other near her home. He tells the constable that she jogged up to him, saying she had been with her mum and now felt too afraid to walk home by herself. I doubt this very much, since she had already walked three-quarters of a mile, quite happily alone. Why would she suddenly be afraid when her home was in sight?

Little tells the young probationer that Rachel asked him to walk with her for her own safety. I smell a very large rat here and don't believe for one second she would do this. At this point, he asked her up to his flat for a drink. No way can I imagine that she would agree to this when her whole intention had been to get home to the kittens as soon as possible. Why would she not go home now, when she was within touching distance of them?

Once again, Little is warned to say no more as he is incriminating himself but he is hell-bent on continuing with this sorry tale. He says that, once inside his flat, he and Rachel started to argue and he 'back-handed' her. She ran into the kitchen and grabbed a small knife that was on top of the refrigerator. She slashed his arm with it and, in retaliation, he took a large knife and stabbed her in her back.

His friend sits through all this in what seemed, says the young PC, shock, horror and amazement. Now Little turns to the probationer and says that he, the friend, had 'nowt to do with it'.

This was his confession, given under caution and no duress. On the way to and after his arrival at the police station, he continues to talk and incriminate himself and eventually signs a statement to this effect.

That Little has since changed this, his original story, does not stop it being used in evidence against him. It came as a great relief when we learned that it would be, though it is of no consolation to us.

One important issue in this statement is that Little admitted immediately that he had stabbed Rachel. At this early stage, nobody was aware of the cause of death. Her body still lay undisturbed in the outside cupboard, awaiting official intervention before it could be removed. Only the person responsible for killing her could know how she had died.

There isn't an awful lot that the defence can say about the PC's version of events, though I am sure Mr Kadri will try. Everything that Little said and owned up to at the time had been noted down and written up in full a very short time afterwards so it will not be easy to dispute. The lead detective had ensured that every little detail was adhered to by the book and as far as I am concerned, the methods used were beyond reproach.

It seems inconceivable that the integrity and honesty of *three* PCs can be called into question but Mr Kadri is not about to give up without a fight. His main argument centres on Little's exoneration of his friend at the scene of crime. The only thing he can do is imply that Little's words were taken out of context, as were the friend's when he asked, 'Do you know anything about this?' Mr Kadri suggests that the tone in which the words were spoken made it not a question at all. That what the friend actually said was, 'You knew about this, didn't you?' and fixed Little with a stare.

Even though his confession cannot now be retracted, Michael Little is at liberty to weave a story around it, to fit the circumstances at hand. He has had long enough to fabricate a story to his advantage.

Thank God, the police team have been so meticulous in their handling of this case. They have done a marvellous job in following up on each and every little detail, leaving no stone unturned, in their efforts to get justice. It will be difficult, if not impossible, for the defence to find any way out for Little. I don't think Mr Kadri scored any points during his cross-examination of the three constables and this is of some comfort.

We are all in need of a short break now, in order to prepare ourselves for this afternoon's two witnesses. They will be, we know, the pathologist, followed by the forensic expert and their evidence will be graphic and traumatic, to say the least. So harrowing will the next few hours be that Ray decides he cannot remain in court to hear their testimony. I fully understand his reluctance, since no father, especially such a doting one, would want to hear what happened to his beloved daughter. Certainly not in lurid detail, in a public arena anyway.

I don't consider myself a harder person but I have a burning need to know as much as possible about Rachel's demise. Only when I know will I be able to put it behind me, as bad as it is. I will sit through it all as it's the very least I can do for her.

To my surprise, the pathologist is a young woman. For some reason, I had expected a man. She is not based in Hull and has travelled some distance to be here today. No nerves as she is sworn in – she is the ultimate professional.

Mr Marson questions her on her findings. She explains that, when she arrived at the crime scene, late on the day of Rachel's discovery, it took some time and planning before her body could be removed from its hiding place.

The exhibits officer produces some bed linen, a blue-coloured sheet and two pillowcases. They look clean and tests have determined that they probably belong to the same set as the duvet cover in which Rachel had been wrapped. No blood was detected on these items. Similarly, when shown a blue shirt that had been found in a black sack in the flat, she found no blood staining on that either. I don't imagine she would, since this shirt is most definitely not the one he was wearing that night! She adds that laundering would not have removed all traces of blood.

Then the question of unprotected sex is raised. It is very difficult for me to listen to this. I dare not glance in Mark's direction, but I can hear him sobbing quietly behind me.

Small bruises were found at the top of Rachel's thighs, as well as some blood, the pathologist says. I have my own opinions as to the reason for the latter.

The jacket is now brought forward for her comments. She has counted 34 cuts in the back, made by a knife but estimates that not all of these penetrated Rachel's body. In some instances, the material had been folded, so the knife merely pierced the double thickness. Rachel was actually stabbed 27 times in all.

I keep thinking of myself frantically dialling her mobile that morning. This horrific act was likely in the process of being committed while I was doing so ...

The pathologist speaks next of her findings inside Little's flat. The beast sits impassively before me, seemingly without a care in the world. How wise Ray is to have avoided this. It is hard enough for me, the supposedly placid one of us two, to remain silent, when every nerve in me is straining to get at Little. To force him to acknowledge what he has done, to show even a vestige of remorse.

It would seem that he did a good job in cleaning up afterwards. That must have been a first for him. Still, even though he had scoured everything thoroughly with strong detergent, blood spots remained. Some were on the wall and more close to his front door, though these were diluted and watery. Tests had proved them to be Rachel's blood. My heart is breaking when I hear that patterns from the soles of Rachel's trainers were evident on that same door, where the majority of blood was found.

This was Rachel's escape route. Only she didn't escape the clutches of Michael Little and his knife. It is not difficult to visualise that she was at the door, trying to get out, when this spineless bastard did what only a complete coward could have done. He stabbed our little girl in her back.

It had to be told and now I know. I know, too, that worse is to come. The forensic scientist has still to give his evidence and, in all probability, it will be even more graphic than that of the pathologist.

Mr Kadri does not question the young woman, for, in reality, he cannot dispute any of her findings. She knows her job and has carried it out flawlessly. She has merely stated the irrefutable facts.

The forensic scientist now takes the stand with great confidence. He is a professor and gives his name, title and qualifications, which are legion and take some time to recite. I am impressed. No doubt he has given evidence on similar occasions and will be aware that the victim's family and loved ones are here today. However, he pulls no punches and does not go out of his way to spare our feelings when he speaks. In his line of work, it is not an option. He cannot let himself become emotionally involved, nor would I expect him to.

As the traumatic details begin to emerge, there is only one way for me to cope. I pretend it is a stranger of whom he speaks. Not Rachel, never my own sweet Rachel.

The professor goes into great detail about the wounds inflicted on her – how he had been able to estimate the angle of penetration, even at which point during the attack she was moving around and which injuries occurred while she was on the ground. The absence of any defence wounds speaks volumes to me.

The first thrusts of the knife were carried out with a great force behind them. Some of the wounds went right through her body and emerged from her chest, severing ribs and vital organs. Eventually, when Rachel lay on the ground and was most probably dead, this unspeakable monster continued to stab her inert body. Sixteen times the knife went into her neck before he was done. He is lower than a snake in the grass, to do that to anybody, least of all our beautiful, inoffensive Rachel, within minutes of encountering her.

It would be so easy for me to break down completely at this moment. Most of all, I wish his mother was sitting here in this court, listening. Would he then, perhaps, show a modicum of shame?

Why did he have to desecrate her graceful, swanlike neck? Had he not done enough when she could no longer struggle? I can think of no word other than 'sub-human' to describe him. I only pray that, when the first blow was struck, Rachel went into such shock that she knew no more.

This has been the worst day so far, with, perhaps, the professor's evidence being the hardest to come to terms with. No less easy, though, were the pathologist's remarks, concerning the state of Rachel's body at first sight. How can I ever close my eyes again without bringing to mind the image of my precious Rachel being trussed up in an old blanket and stashed away like so much garbage. She had been left so long there, doubled over, that she had started to mummify. So long that fungus had grown all over and around her and her eyes, those big blue eyes, had dried and shrivelled up. Dear God, what did she ever do to deserve such a fate? The indignity that she suffered is almost too much to bear. None of us can stand much more of this day.

I thank God that Ray chose not to sit through the events of this afternoon. I fear it would have broken him entirely and irreversibly. Thank goodness, too, for the support of so many, though some of Rachel's immediate family and friends could not stomach all the gory details. They had to leave the courtroom in some distress.

I'm sure that Ronnie – Ray's only brother and Rachel's uncle – never thought he would experience this day. Not in his wildest dreams could he have envisioned how her life would end, when, on the day of her baptism, he became her godfather. He is truly heartbroken, both for what fate befell his much-loved niece and no less, I imagine, for his brother, my husband of 40 years. Michael Little does not realise how very lucky he is to be shielded from the public gallery behind toughened glass.

As for Saoirse, Rachel's best and oldest friend, there are no words to describe her sorrow. Is she recalling, I wonder, those happy, childhood days when they were school chums and dancing partners? And the later years of young womanhood, when they would paint the town and have sleepovers? Rachel would be so touched to know that Saoirse is still here for her, even now.

One of the few satisfactions today was the professor's certainty that there was absolutely no sign of any drugs in Rachel's system. Not that we believed there would be but rumours had reached us in the early days. People were looking for reasons and for it to be drug-related was an easy option.

It is a mercy too at the end of this day that the trial is being held in our home town. We need do no more than drive the short distance home before collapsing. Heaven help those who do not have this luxury. How does anyone cope with the stress of a day such as this and then face the prospect of driving a long way home? I really feel for those who have had to do it and those who may yet have to. Judge Hooper did us a real service when he ruled that this trial would be held in Hull.

Friday, 17 October 2003
– Day Four

Today will see the end of this first week. It seems to be going well for us so far and all concerned – barristers, CPS and police – are all quietly satisfied with the progress made.

There have been occasions when frustration has set in. We, or the jury or sometimes the press, have been asked to leave the courtroom during legal debates. However, we had been forewarned to expect this kind of thing, so we are not unduly worried. This morning some discussion takes place in hushed tones between Mr Marson and the judge before Little is even brought into the court. Soon afterwards, we are all asked to vacate the court.

On our return, we learn that a warrant has been produced for Marc Fuller, the lad at Little's flat on the day of the arrest. It is quite an unexpected turn of events and rather worrying. We don't know if, or when, Marc will be located. If he does make an appearance, will his evidence help or hinder the case? I am fearful but can do no more than wait and hope.

Our liquid lunches continue. It is quite out of character for most of us, but in this strange new world in which we find ourselves everything has a dreamlike quality to it. We are just not the same people we were this time last year. How could we be? Never in our wildest dreams could we have imagined ourselves in this situation. Rachel herself would be shocked rigid at all of this but we are living it and must see it through to the bitter end.

When we return to court one, we learn that Marc will indeed put in an appearance today. Not only that, but his mother and sister will also be witnesses for the prosecution. The police have no doubt that Marc was in no way connected with Rachel or her murder and any suggestion to the contrary would be dismissed. Some of his family members will travel from Scotland. We also hear that one person will be coming over from Spain next week. We are astonished to learn of these further witnesses.

Marc's evidence could be crucial in putting Little's yarns into disrepute. The prosecution insist that Little's first version of events is the only true one, the one that lays the blame purely at his own feet and exonerates Marc. Their job is to prove this version while, at the same time, disproving all the other ones. They have to prove Michael Little guilty, whereas the defence do not have to prove his innocence.

This is a frightening and, to my mind, most unfair aspect of the British legal system. The defence must be given every scrap of evidence as it emerges, but they need not reciprocate. It gives the accused an advantage since he can be told what the prosecution has against him and thus is able to act upon every allegation. Since trials such as this one take many months to come to court, so the accused has ample time in which to build up a plausible story in his defence, to cover every eventuality.

It would seem that Little has taken full advantage of this rather precarious point of law. Back in April when DNA results were returned, proving without a shadow of a doubt that he had had sex with Rachel, a rethink was required. Until that point, he had never mentioned that this act had taken place. Perhaps he thought that it would remain undetected, that such evidence would have disappeared due to the length of time Rachel had lain in the cupboard. How wrong he was.

Between then and his plea and directions hearing in May, a second defence statement was conjured up. As expected, he did not enter a plea on 2 May. Instead, he was granted a further three weeks in which to put together his story. So it was that, at the end of that month, he pleaded not guilty on the grounds that a third party was to be implicated and that this third party was, in fact, the murderer, though he did have consensual sex with Rachel. That much he couldn't now refute.

Marc has now arrived in court. We know he is here because the media have informed us. We are all nervous and we wonder what will happen. There has been so much damning evidence against Little that there can be no real reason to worry. Marc's evidence can only compound the case against Little. The fact that Little has already made it clear that Marc was in no way involved and that Little has signed his own confession and been seen on CCTV at the relevant time must surely be enough to condemn him?

An independent doctor, at the time of the arrest, could find no trace of a wound on Little, thus refuting the claim that Rachel had cut his arm. As well as this, we have heard the evidence of the three constables and the partygoers that night, all of which put Little's later defence statements into disrepute. What, in the face of all this evidence, should we have to fear? Surely Marc's evidence can only help us more?

The police have no doubt that Marc's alibi is concrete and they put much effort into proving it. We put our trust in the police even while realising that the defence could yet put a spanner in the works. No doubt they have further tricks up their sleeves but what these tricks are, we have no way of knowing.

Marc takes his place on the stand and it is plain for all to see he is a *very* hostile witness. He repeats the oath and begins to speak. His words are littered with expletives even when he is questioned first by Mr Marson, the prosecution barrister.

Oh my God! This is dreadful to behold. What will the jury think of his outbursts, his anger and his disrespectful attitude? Marc is terrified and therefore furious. If this is how he is reacting when quizzed by the prosecution, how will he conduct himself when confronted by the defence? He will be fair game to Mr Kadri and I must leave the courtroom following this exchange with our own barrister. I know that I will be unable to watch while this vulnerable young man is torn to shreds by Mr Kadri, a very experienced barrister. I am afraid that, in his current mood, Marc will blow his top completely. I have no wish to witness what might happen then.

Later, when I am joined on the concourse by some of the others, I learn that sparks really flew during the heated exchanges that took place. Marc caused quite a few raised eyebrows with his language but he held his own very well under intense pressure from the defence. The police are pleased and relieved at how he came across and I understand that there were a few light-hearted moments.

I ask to meet Marc, in order to express our thanks for what he has done today. Marc is in a small private room and I am told he is extremely upset. I can only see him if he agrees to it and I ask the DC in charge to pass on our thanks, should Marc not wish to see me. Maybe this works, because I am quickly taken to where he is and Vanda joins us after a few moments. All of his previous bravado is gone and he is crying his eyes out. My heart goes out to him and Vanda and I thank him profusely for being here. I add that, had he and Rachel ever met, they would have got on very well. This merely serves to upset him even more. I whisper to him that I know for certain that he is in no way connected to Rachel's death.

Even without Little's own confession, without the weight of evidence stacked up against him and aside from my own recognition of him, I know, with a gut feeling, that he is the one. The same gut feeling that tells me Marc is not involved at all.

Court is about to convene once more and some of his family are to be called as witnesses for the prosecution. I am anxious to hear what they have to say. Marc's mother and sister are expected to appear first and no doubt they are every bit as afraid as he was when he took the stand. Were he a son of mine, I would be scared stiff knowing, as I am sure they must, what he is now being accused of. Do they know, I wonder, that the defence are trying to place Marc in the frame by means of the CCTV footage taken from the supermarket, as a means of backing up Little's allegations?

The image of a young man they have isolated is shown to Marc's mum and later his sister. Both deny that it is him and both are questioned in depth as to how they are so certain of this. It seems to me that the defence, in their desperation, are simply clutching at straws and my suspicions are further roused when the time comes up on the screen. The figure in question appears before 1am and sits on a nearby electricity supply box for ten minutes doing nothing in particular. When the tape is forwarded, it shows this same person get up and saunter away in the opposite direction. The defence allege that it was Marc and that was the spot where he was waiting to meet Rachel in order to hand over cannabis. It was a drug deal that was to go wrong and Marc was the killer. Pure fiction which the jury had no trouble disregarding. Apart from anything else, the forensic evidence demonstrated beyond doubt that no drugs were involved.

The figure on the screen is a noticeably shorter person and the clothing does not correspond to what Marc is said to have been wearing that night. It could have been anyone but for sure, it isn't Marc. Are we seriously expected to believe that this person, whoever it was, loitered around for an hour and did not encounter either Rachel or Little on their way home? Since it was around 2am, not 1am, when they were captured on this same camera, with nobody else nearby at the time, it is hard to believe that this person is of any significance whatsoever.

Further evidence from Marc's family would seem to back up the idea that he could not have been anywhere near that spot at 1am that morning. Phone records from his home that night prove that calls came in from Scotland and North Yorkshire. These were timed at just after midnight and then 15 minutes later and, in each case, it was Marc who answered the telephone before passing it on to his mother. His mother, sister and consequent witnesses state this to be true. I do not consider for one moment that they are all lying, since this has been their evidence from the very start, even before Little changed his story. They are therefore not just making this up; their original statements were made way back in February.

I feel that the defence are particularly harsh and scathing towards both mother and sister, neither of whom shares Marc's anger, or his strong language! They both retire in tears at the end of a lengthy grilling at the hands of Mr Kadri.

He is not so vitriolic towards the two uncles from whom the telephone calls had been received that night, as the timing of the calls cannot be disputed. He still insists, however, that Marc could have left the house afterwards and arrived at the spot in question before 1am, though I fail to see how.

Michael Little and his counsel are using the full letter of the law to their advantage. It is their prerogative to keep back whatever they wish.

It is beyond comprehension that, having already confessed to Rachel's killing, the odds continue to be stacked in Little's favour. Instead of her being the victim, he remains innocent until proven guilty. Meanwhile, he is able to pull every trick in the book in pursuit of freedom. How can that be fair?

On a scale of one to ten, this was not the worst of days, but bad enough. We are all looking forward to a little respite over the weekend and the chance to recharge our batteries, ready for what still lies ahead.

Saturday, 18 October 2003

I do very little today. I feel lethargic and nothing seems of great importance right now. Everything has come to a standstill while the trial is ongoing.

Ray and his brother are together here today and watch some horseracing on the television to while away the hours. I am concerned that Ronnie is missing his wife and family back home in Wicklow. They are not used to him being absent for any length of time, but he is in constant touch by telephone.

Our plan is to eat out this evening. I am sure Ronnie is starving. He is a giant of a man with an appetite to match, normally. I haven't been the best or most conscientious of hostesses up to now. Ray goes out to fetch the local evening paper and what a shock! After a lot of coverage yesterday, we weren't expecting anything further over the weekend. How wrong we were. A picture of Marc Fuller takes up much of the front page with the headline: WAS THIS MAN THE KILLER?

We read on and are stunned to see how the media have reported the case. We feel very let down that they have chosen to do this, even though they are entitled to report things in whatever way they please. It seems to be pure sensationalism but it is very unfair to Marc and it seems to us to be a travesty. It is very disappointing for us, after so much good publicity has gone before. We can hardly believe that our own local newspaper would do this. It is almost like a betrayal.

Not only that, it is grossly unfair to Marc to use these particular words, since he has done nothing wrong. He has never been considered a suspect nor charged with any offence. I wonder how he and his family will feel should they see this story. Very uncomfortable, I would imagine.

Perhaps there will be no respite for us this weekend after all. This article can only damage the case.

Monday, 20 October 2003
– Day Five

The first day of the second week arrives. Dare we hope that this trial may be over before the weekend? Our team certainly seem to think so, but we do not know what today has in store for us.

Friday was dramatic, with Mr Kadri's accusation that Marc was the real killer, a claim strenuously denied by the lad. Given the CCTV footage that the defence says is Marc, plus the indisputable telephone calls from his family and the timing of them, it is impossible that he could have got from his house to the place in question in such a short space of time. It is a distance of almost six miles and he had no transport of any kind. As Marc himself said, he is no Olympic athlete!

This, however, was not enough to satisfy the defence team, who demanded that maps and further film be made of the route to back up their claim. The latter request has been undertaken over the weekend by a DC. Maps are reproduced to a larger scale.

Using two separate routes, the officer walked at a brisk pace from Marc's home to where the camera is situated. The first journey covered 5.56 miles and took one hour and 40 minutes and the second covered 5.65 miles and took him one hour and 45 minutes. The route via our house is even further. Marc could not possibly have done it on foot, nor could many others I suspect. I hope that the jury are as convinced by this as we are.

Today we hear more evidence that demonstrates the absurdity of the defence allegations. It comes from a Spanish gentleman who was staying with Marc's family over the New Year period. He backs up the claim that Marc was indeed in the house soon after midnight on the relevant night, that two phone calls were answered by Marc between 12.05 and 12.17am, and that he then passed the receiver to his mother. He also says he was still in the house the following morning, when the household arose. Will this be enough to dispel all doubt, despite the adverse press coverage and Mr Kadri's valiant attempts to muddy the waters?

Later, evidence is given by a chap brought into court in handcuffs. He has come from the local prison. He had been before the magistrate on the same day that Little was initially charged with Rachel's murder and shared a holding cell with him. This man is classed as an habitual criminal but his previous convictions do not include physical violence. He has never killed anybody but, like most other prison inmates, he patently holds a dim view of offenders like Michael Little.

His testimony is that, when he asked Little what the charge against him was, Little had replied, 'Murder.' Rachel's name came into the conversation and, for some reason, the two became involved in a scuffle, which was later reported by the prison authorities. It was at this point that A, as I shall call him, agreed to come to court and repeat what had been said. I think he is very brave to do this, having heard how other prisoners take against those who help the police. He had nothing to gain but plenty to lose by being here today. He will certainly gain no remission as his sentence is all but over anyway.

A alleges that Little, when asked at first why he had done it (killed Rachel), did not reply. Later, he told A that it was an accident, that he was drunk and it was an argument that went wrong. When asked what he had done with her body, he said that he had 'stuck it in a cupboard'. How chilling to hear these words. How very cold-blooded is this butcher to speak so of our Rachel, so loved and cherished, as if she was a piece of garbage to be thrown away out of sight.

Mr Kadri tries to make short work of A, belittling the word of a criminal, an obvious liar and therefore untrustworthy as far as he is concerned. However, A is a different kettle of fish to previous witnesses. He has been before such men as Mr Kadri many times before and is unfazed by his suggestions and attempts to discredit him. He stands up to the defence very well indeed, as does a PC who is called to the stand afterwards to give his evidence.

This constable had been escorting Little during a transfer some weeks after his arrest, during which time Little tried to engage him in conversation. He told this PC that his reason for remaining silent, his constant 'no comment' plea, was because he was protecting someone. I daresay by then he had been concocting his plan to incriminate an innocent third party and perhaps thought these words would sow seeds of doubt in the minds of the police. However, this very astute officer, to his credit and integrity, did not take the bait. He merely noted down the conversations and reported them, which is why he is here today. I cannot praise the police force highly enough, each and every officer involved in the case. They have been so professional and done every little thing by the book.

By now, we are all feeling the effects of the previous week and are exhausted. When we reach home each evening, we cannot find the energy or the incentive to do anything at all. Today is no different. We have a lot to think about this night because we heard, late today, that Little himself will take the stand tomorrow! Mr Marson cannot wait to begin his questioning and I echo his sentiments entirely.

Tuesday, 21 October 2003
– Day Six

This is the moment we have been waiting for and all that has kept me going through these long, dark months. In fact, I didn't dare believe that it would actually happen. I never thought this fiend would have the courage to face us all in an open court, but face us he must, the only witness in his own defence. It says a lot that not one person has come forward to speak up on his behalf, nor has any family member or friend appeared to support him.

Just before 11am, we hear the announcement over the tannoy. 'All interested parties in the case of Michael Little, please proceed to court one.'

It is the moment!

For the first time, we come within touching distance of this aberration as he lumbers up to the stand to give his evidence. Were I in his shoes, I would be quaking with fear, having to walk past the public gallery, packed as it is with Rachel's family and friends. However, if he is nervous, he hides it well. If anything, he looks decidedly smug. We shall soon see whether that changes under pressure.

Two burly security guards sit close to him as he takes the oath in a hesitant, high-pitched voice, one that belies his massive bulk. Mr Kadri, as the defending counsel, will begin the questioning and no doubt treat him with kid gloves.

Whatever initial confidence Little may have shown begins to wane quickly. His voice shakes and is such that he can scarcely be heard at times, which prompts both the judge and Mr Kadri to ask him to slow down and to speak up. This seems to unnerve him somewhat. I am highly gratified to note this and hope it is a sign of things to come.

He is asked about his one-time friendship with Nathan Tempest (the first witness for the prosecution), who was his temporary flatmate. Points are raised regarding his penchant for smoking cannabis and his drinking habits. He admits to the use of LSD, amphetamines and the drug ecstasy, then adds that he suffers from 'clinical depression', for which he takes medication.

Clinical depression, my arse, is what crosses my mind at these pathetic words. Who in this life does not get depressed, yet does not go on to commit murder?

Little goes on to list various other medical complaints he claims to suffer from, including the effects of two cycling accidents he had at a younger age.

He is obviously trying to drum up as much sympathy as he can for himself, in order to come across as a pitiful individual. We have been warned that he would do this, so we are not surprised, nor are we fooled. None of us in the public gallery takes our eyes off him, but he does not return our gaze. No doubt he has been told not to by whoever has briefed him beforehand. We are scandalised to see him bring out a rosary from under his shirt. What a charlatan! He clearly does not know that a true Catholic would never wear these around the neck; they are normally held in the hands. I feel bitter to think that any priest might have given them to him.

I verge between fascination and hysteria as I listen to them. Not only is Little's story shocking, but if it were a film it would be laughed out of the cinema! Sadly, this is no laughing matter; my daughter's reputation is at stake. Still, he is fighting for his life, so I guess anything goes.

Little tells the jury that, on the night in question, he left the party much later than previous witnesses had testified. Are they liars then? His route home, he says, did not take him past our house, even though he had initially admitted it did, even said that he had seen two females in conversation outside of this address! He goes on to say the journey – a distance of less than three miles – took him several hours. Very hard to believe.

His reasons why the journey took so long are that he doesn't walk too well due to an old injury and that, although not drunk, he had to stop no less than ten times to be sick! Despite his malaise, he was well enough to stop to buy a pizza, though where he found an establishment open for business at this hour is anyone's guess. Did anyone check the validity of this statement, I wonder? He was also able to telephone his mother on his way home, despite his claim that he had only three 5p pieces in his pocket. Maybe he used his mobile, then, or maybe he didn't ring her at all.

Although he himself does not mention it, his erstwhile friend, Nathan Tempest, testified that Little had told him he had found a £10 note while walking home that morning. I am beside myself with rage, looking at him now and knowing this. Could this, by any chance, be the £10 that Rachel's father had given her? Of course it was, because he didn't 'find it'. He stole it from her dead body, together with her lighter and ever-present Lambert & Butler, which were never recovered.

I find it galling to listen to his words, knowing that I could have given evidence of having seen him at 1.50am that morning, thus refuting his claims. I could also have added that, when he walked by Rachel and me, his clothing showed no sign of persistent vomiting. He looked perfectly clean and respectable. Had he not done so, I would never have entertained the idea of asking him to walk along with her, as I had briefly considered doing.

The scene is set now for Little's arrival home, where he says he found his old school friend, Marc Fuller, already ensconced in the flat. With him was a female, hitherto unknown to him. This strange state of affairs came as no surprise to Little. He didn't ask what they were doing there, though most people would have done. No introductions were requested or made. Little merely went into his bedroom, changed out of his 'messed-up' clothes and made himself a cup of coffee.

Am I alone in thinking this behaviour very odd? How many folk would act in such a nonchalant manner, having entered their own home in the early hours of the morning to discover a seldom-seen friend already there? Not to mention an unknown girl with him. Little admits that such a thing had never happened before, so surely some explanation would be called for?

Little next alleges that, having changed his clothes, he joined the two of them and asked Marc to introduce him to his guest. Marc, however, did not know who she was either, even though we are expected to believe he contacted her earlier to sell her some cannabis. The girl said that her name was Rachel. According to Little, she and Marc were drinking and talking; he had lager, while Rachel was sipping alcopops.

First big mistake, Little. Rachel never, ever drank that sort of thing. In fact, she rarely drank at all, except on special occasions. Would she have been sitting happily in a stranger's house – a filthy, unkempt one at that – with a person she had supposedly met for the first time on the street that night? I think not.

Further, if any of this were remotely true, if she was there of her own free will, Rachel would have had no reason at all not to answer her mobile phone that night.

Little goes on to say that Rachel wished him Happy New Year and then they started to discuss his video collection. He proudly states that he has about 200, not bad going for someone who has never held down a job! How gratifying to know that my tax is paying towards his luxuries.

Little makes his next mistake by saying that Rachel asked him if he had a BMX racing game. She had never been known to have an interest in the subject. WWF wrestling, perhaps, or music, but BMX – never! Who does he think he is kidding?

Mr Kadri asks him what happened next and I can barely contain myself when I hear his reply. Little claims that he went into his bedroom to find the BMX game, only to realise that Rachel had come in after him. He was most surprised by this. She was standing behind him and asked if he thought she was good looking.

What a load of crap! Rachel would never have asked anyone

that question. She was the least vain person one could ever meet, had no idea of how stunning she was and, what's more, cared even less.

When asked what his reply was, Michael Little, this most versatile of actors, smiles and says that he told her she was 'extremely gorgeous'. At which, Rachel put her arms around his neck and they began kissing.

No, no, no! That would never have happened! I know my daughter too well and she was no slut. She had only ever had one boyfriend, and him for almost three years. She would never, ever have gone off with anyone on a whim, not that night, not ever. Least of all with the likes of Little, who represented everything she detested in a male.

Who does this repulsive creature think he is? Apart from being grossly obese, he has nondescript features and patently verges on being completely moronic. I can think of few girls who would find him attractive and Rachel would definitely not have been one of them.

What this vile individual alleges happened next leaves poor Mark inconsolable. How dare this bastard heap even more coals on the head of someone who is so bereft and distraught? Not to mention us, her parents, the rest of her family and her friends. In his bid for freedom, he is sullying the memory of a beautiful, innocent girl, putting her reputation into disrepute. It is so very, very hard to listen to this and not to shout out against it.

He continues that one thing led to another and they ended up having sex.

In his dreams! He could never aspire to a girl like Rachel, nor any other girl, I would imagine, for that matter. Unless he took her by force. Rachel did not have unprotected sex with

Mark, her boyfriend, so why would she with Little? According to him, shortly after this act, Marc came storming into the room. He who had said and done nothing while this act was being perpetrated, even though he was only on the other side of the open door. He would have heard everything, had it actually happened at all.

Supposedly, Marc was totally out of control when he burst into the room and found the two of them together. He called Little a traitor and swore at him, saying that Rachel was *his*. In his own imagination, I would guess that this is a fantasy he has lived out many times: the good guy gets the beautiful girl while the bad guy is thwarted at every turn.

At this altercation, he claims, Rachel came out of the bedroom and said, 'I'm nobody's!' Now where have I heard that line before? Could it have been Michelle Pfeiffer in *The Fabulous Baker Boys*? This saga is becoming more unbelievable by the minute and, were it not so tragic, I would laugh out loud! Surely no sane person will believe it? This is all so very painful for each of us.

Little carries on. Marc is totally out of control now. He goes berserk and grabs a knife from inside the kitchen. Strange that he could accomplish this at such speed and be able to lay his hand on one so effortlessly. I would find it difficult in my own kitchen!

Little admits to having a block of such knives, plus several more around his flat. How weird is that, when this animal lived on junk food and takeaways? For what purpose did he require sharp kitchen knives? Certainly not to cook with, anyway.

Little continues that Marc started to make slashing motions with the knife while swearing and cursing at Little, at which point Rachel took control. She kept grabbing Little and telling him to go back into the bedroom and she would 'sort it out'. As if!

Rachel, who according to Little's own testimony did not know either of these two men, would have done no such thing. Nor, I suspect, would any sane person on seeing a knife being wielded in this manner. She would have run for her life, had she been able to. If indeed it had really happened like that. So would the cowardly Michael Little!

Choking back crocodile tears, he continues, as Ray sits with eyes closed and John with head bowed. Neither can bear to look at Little. What an actor. What a fantasist. I wonder how many times he has rehearsed this scene to make the greatest impact.

Mr Kadri gently asks him what then occurred and he affects a few more tears before going on with what could surely have him nominated for an Oscar. Marc, he says, lunged forward with the knife and connected with Rachel. He brought the knife back and forth and just 'went crazy'. He doesn't know how many times she was stabbed, but the point came where she fell to the floor at Little's feet. Marc allegedly then knelt and straddled Rachel's body and continued to stab her in the neck, all the while calling her a bitch.

This account is too graphic and too real for it not to be true. I have no doubt that Rachel did meet her end in this way and that every little detail is still retained in Little's mind. I am sure, too, that he did watch her as she kicked her legs against the door as her life ebbed away, trying in vain to escape the knife which her murderer still brandished as he loomed over her. Only the one who had committed this crime could recall it in such fine detail. All the rest is a figment of his twisted imagination.

Mr Kadri looks across the courtroom, as if he is assessing the jury's reaction, before continuing. Has he heard all or any of this before, one could wonder, and, if so, what does he really think of his client? This hasn't been his first story, or his second, or even his third!

Little's narrative is not yet over and, in disbelief, we hear the final twist in the tale. This is the bit which he has added as a recent afterthought and which, no doubt, he hopes will be his trump card.

Still totally manic, Marc apparently turned to him and said that it was Little who he had really wanted to kill, and not Rachel. Now it was all Little's fault that she was dead. He could easily kill him too but would not because, were he to do so, there would be not one, but two bodies. If the police turned up, they would know that it was Marc who was the killer! I don't believe I am hearing this. I can only say that he has missed out on his true vocation – he ought to become an author of fiction.

With Rachel's body lying on the floor and the obviously huge amount of blood involved, Marc next ordered Little to get to work. He threw a towel to him and told him to clean things up, before warning him of the consequences should he ever tell anyone what had happened. Were he to do so, Marc would come after not only him, but also his entire family. A total fabrication, only brought into play at the eleventh hour, so denying the police the opportunity to investigate and act upon this allegation. They would certainly have kept Little's family under surveillance, as well as monitoring Marc's telephone and his movements, had they been made aware of any such threats.

Is Michael Little, as has been suggested, inadequate?

No, he is merely as sly and cunning as a fox — a fact I have long suspected.

The hour break for lunch is nerve-wracking and I can eat nothing at all. I am just too nervous at the thought of this afternoon's confrontation between our barrister and Little. Ideally, I would like to think he will get some answers for us during his questioning but that is rather a forlorn hope. Little is sticking to his story so I cannot imagine he will crack now and tell the truth. No Perry Mason-type showdowns likely in court one. That would be too much to ask but I have great faith in Mr Marson's ability. I know he will do his level best for us.

Back into the courtroom, we all rise for the judge. Little has obviously been well schooled; he never fails to bow his head in reverence on these occasions! He must want to come across as a servile, law-abiding citizen but we are not taken in, and especially not by the rosary. Little is led to the stand and Mr Marson is ready for him. The cross-examination will begin and a mass of butterflies take flight in my stomach. I am shaking now in anticipation of what may ensue.

It starts amicably, as Mr Marson turns and nods to the back of the courtroom. The exhibits officer approaches and hands him a couple of knives, protected in see-through cylindrical covers. He takes one of them and says dramatically, 'Is this the knife that killed Rachel Moran?'

Little gives it a cursory glance before replying in the negative.

'Is it *like* the knife that killed her?'

'Yes.'

A second knife is handed to Mr Marson. To me, they seem identical, both horrifying to behold, being large, lethal and vicious-looking. A shiver runs down my spine at the sight of what my daughter must have faced just before she died. Little agrees that this is the knife that killed Rachel, though how he can assert this with such certainty when they are so similar is anyone's guess. From the evidence of the pathologist, we know that blood was found on only one of the knives recovered from Little's flat. In my own mind, I am sure that he was privy to that information and even to which knife it was. He agrees that both knives came from the block of five he kept in his kitchen.

Oh, Rachel, my poor, poor girl. What horrors did you have to endure before your life was snuffed out with such savagery by this butcher? Until I saw this murderous weapon, I had blocked my mind to its existence. That way, I did not have to dwell on your final moments of terror.

In a quiet yet menacing voice, Mr Marson continues, 'You killed Rachel, didn't you?'

Little: 'No.'

'You are evil.'

'No.'

A slight pause. 'Do you agree that the person who killed Rachel is evil?'

'Yes.'

'Do you agree that the person who stabbed Rachel did it deliberately and with the intention of killing her?'

'Yes, it was Marc.'

A further pause. 'But it was a wicked thing that you did, in concealing her body all that time.'

'Yes.'

'During that time, did you ever think of what her family were going through?'

'Yes.'

'Why, then, didn't you do something about it?'

With eyes lowered, Little half whispers, 'Because of my own guilt.'

Even though I am sure he has heard this, Mr Marson asks Little to repeat what he has just said.

'My own guilt.'

Raising his voice now, Mr Marson almost shouts, 'What did *you* have to be guilty about?'

'That I didn't help Rachel.'

So now he is putting the onus on himself, is he? Sorry, Michael Little, but we don't believe you. The only person you want to help is yourself.

Mr Marson is just getting started and we see him in a new light as he presses on. No kid-glove treatment from him as he attempts to portray Little in his true colours!

The difference in his approach to every witness compared to that of the defence is marked. Indeed, he is a totally different character to Mr Kadri. We abhor the task he has taken on in defending Little and for that reason alone, rightly or wrongly, it is difficult to look upon him in a kindly light, even though someone had to take the job on.

Mr Marson is the quintessential Englishman: cool, calm and collected. He has perfect, precise diction and never, would I imagine, does he open his mouth without knowing exactly what his next words will be.

His *modus operandi* comes to the fore now as his cross-examination continues, taking apart all that Little purports to be true, making him squirm like a worm on a hook. Were it anybody else, I could feel quite sorry for them, but, under the circumstances, I find it quite gratifying to see this excuse for a man being cut down to size. He has more than met his match in Mr Marson and finally seems to have lost his complacency.

His nervousness shows as he blinks rapidly and constantly licks his lips, hesitating and stumbling over his words. All the while he is trying to keep one step ahead of Mr Marson but usually failing miserably.

He is challenged about the clothing he says Marc wore on New Year's Eve and almost loses the plot. He disputes that he was only able to identify the type and colour of Marc's clothes after seeing the CCTV footage of the person alleged to be Marc. He becomes agitated, denying it and saying he told his solicitor beforehand. Because he had been able to see the film in question before it was shown in court, I feel that Mr Marson's accusation is right

Mr Marson: 'Why didn't you give the description of Marc's clothing to the police then?'

Little: 'Because they never asked me to.'

A glance towards the police bench seems to imply that this is a downright lie. They all look to each other in amazement, seemingly angry, as I am.

Where is the fairness in all of this when my request to see the footage of Little, in order to confirm my suspicions, was denied? I wanted no more than to ascertain in my own mind that it had been him who had walked by me earlier. It would have made absolutely no difference to my evidence but was disallowed anyway. Clearly, the defence do not have to adhere to the same laws of practice as do the prosecution.

It is satisfying to see Little contradicting himself now and eventually conceding that he could be wrong in his identification of Marc on the CCTV film. He still has to add, however, 'But it looks quite like him.'

There are some problems when he is asked about a statement he had signed back in June. Standing his ground, he claims not to remember it. It's rather embarrassing when this document is produced for his perusal, as it soon becomes obvious that he can't read it. Mr Marson tries to force the issue and Little has to admit that his reading skills are poor. We shouldn't be surprised that he is semi-literate but somehow, it is another blow that the person who took Rachel's life is one of this calibre.

Inevitably, the phone calls I made to Rachel are brought up.

Mr Marson: 'What happened when Rachel's telephone rang?'

Little: 'It didn't ring when I was there.'

'But you have heard the evidence of Rachel's mother. She said that she rang continuously, from 2.30am until almost 4.00am! How do you explain that?'

'It didn't ring at all.'

How dare he lie without changing his expression? How dare he imply that I invented those calls, when the SIM card from Rachel's mobile has already proved my words to be true? Each call, the time it was made, the duration of the calls and even the final one, they were all logged; even the one that was terminated when someone switched off the phone. He heard them. Of course he heard them, for he was the one who eventually turned the phone off – probably after he had killed Rachel. I just pray that she didn't hear the phone and know that help was just at the other end of the line. I hope that she was already dead by the time I first called her. The alternative does not bear thinking about.

Can I even listen as Little shamelessly goes into detail of how Rachel was disposed of? How he left her in his bathroom while he scrubbed the place clean, even though he

Rachel with my younger brother, her uncle Allan, who also died far too young under tragic circumstances.

Rachel with Ray and I on holiday when she was about 15 in Glendalough, Ireland.

Top: Rachel with Vanda.

Bottom: Standing over her brother John and Vanda.

On holiday in America in the summer of 2000 – wearing her WWF wrestling gear!

Top: In our garden aged about 18.

Bottom: Rachel with her brother John on 30 December 1999.

In her own flat with Speedy Tomato the kitten!

Top: Rachel with her boyfriend Mark in 2002.

Bottom: This is her last ever picture. She has very blonde hair here. It was taken in the pub with a friend on 31 December 2003. A few hours later she was dead.

This was 2003, the year of Rachel's death. She was 21. We didn't realise we had this picture until the police asked us for a snap. Her brother John found a film which hadn't been developed in his camera and this was among the photos. It became iconic in the press in the months afterwards and is the image that was used to paint her portrait.

insists that it was Marc who made him do it? He makes no mention of where Marc was during this time, or whether the cleaning took place before or after Rachel was bundled into the cupboard.

He shows no emotion when asked who disposed of her belongings. He replies that it was he alone. He went to the drain during the early hours of that same morning and threw Rachel's meagre possessions into the water. I was probably still sitting around, waiting for her to call, trying to contact her, while he was doing this. Now I know why I had such a strong feeling of foreboding at that time. Call it intuition or a mother's sixth sense, but I knew, just knew, that something very bad had happened to Rachel even then.

Much of this testimony has been given once already to the defence lawyer during his questioning of Little. Hearing it repeated does not make it any easier to accept. Perhaps the most heartbreaking moment is when Little relates his version of what occurred as Rachel fell to the floor in her final death throes.

Mr Marson: 'Did Rachel say anything as she was falling?'
Little: 'Yes, she said something.'
'What did she say?'
'She said something, but I couldn't understand her.'

Oh, God, for one terrible moment, my heart stands still. I was so sure that he was going to say she had called out for one of us. Had that been so, that would have been the end of me, but Little's words haunt me anyway. Common sense tells me that she most probably said nothing, that what he heard was no more than her final breath leaving her body. But I will never know for sure and I shall always wonder.

As far as the allegation that Marc was dominating him is

concerned, can it just be me who finds that hard to believe? We have seen these two men in court: Little, at 16 stone plus, is built like a gorilla, while Marc has the physique of a whippet. I do not, for one second, accept that Little was ever afraid of him, and by what means could he have been terrorised? And not only him, but also his entire family? Did Marc intend killing them one by one? Does Michael Little really think that anyone will fall for this fantasy?

If his allegations were even halfway true, he had ample opportunity to divulge his fears to the police. A person frightened for his life would have done just that but he instead carried on with his life for a whole month, knowing that Rachel was lying mere feet away from where he ate, slept and no doubt played with his vast array of video games. He went out drinking around the town during that time on more than one occasion and even went and had another tattoo done on his arm. Does this sound like a man who is living in fear? I think not.

Once in custody, and safe from Marc's clutches, he had nothing to lose by disclosing his fears. He posed no threat then, real or imaginary, not to him, nor any of his family, since he was locked up. If Little had genuinely believed his family was in danger, that was the time he should have alerted the police so that they could have protected them. The reason why he didn't do so is because his whole defence is a tissue of lies, from start to finish. The crime he committed was evil to the extreme but what he is further trying to do could be considered, by some, to be equally so.

Mr Marson is not finished with Little. There is still the question of him admitting to walking past our house and seeing two females in conversation on New Year's morning.

Nothing much has been said about this particular aspect of the case thus far. Certainly, it wasn't mentioned during Mr Kadri's questioning of Little. Maybe they hoped it would be discarded when the defence statement kept changing.

Mr Marson, however, has not forgotten this admission and asks Little, 'Why did you first say that you walked home along Hall Road then later say that you didn't?'

Little: 'Because I was told that it wasn't relevant.'

'What do you mean, it wasn't relevant?'

'My solicitor said that the route I took home was not relevant.'

I find the logic behind this hard to follow. Surely his route home was very relevant, given the fact that it was on this very road that Little was captured on CCTV, even though he denies it now. I don't know if I believe any solicitor would advise him to say such a thing, if indeed he did!

It seems, though, that Michael Little is intent on blaming someone, anyone, other than himself, for this situation in which he now finds himself. It looks like his solicitor has drawn the short straw in this instance.

Apart from his initial admissions at the scene of the crime and his willingness to keep talking non-stop until the arrival of his brief, Little didn't answer any questions at all after that. His stock reply to everything put to him was 'No comment'. When asked by Mr Marson why he had not co-operated with the police on any occasion, why he had answered each query with 'No comment', Little replies, 'Because my solicitor told me to.' Well, perhaps he is telling the truth about this, who knows? There is no sign of a solicitor here in court to either back up or refute Little's claims.

It is almost over now, but not quite. Little now has to explain to Mr Marson how Rachel's body ended up in the cupboard, folded and wrapped like a parcel. Again, as before, he alleges that it was done with the aid of Marc. He couldn't have done such a thing alone. His words precisely were, 'I may be big but I'm not strong. I have a messed-up shoulder.'

At 16 stone, compared to Rachel's nine, he would be more than capable of such a feat, of that I am certain. Even I could have lifted and carried her, should the need ever have arisen. Before he stands down, he tells the court that he is 'not a violent person' (not while he is here today anyway!). As he is led away, to be taken back to the dock, he appears to limp past the public gallery – an affectation that has not been seen so far but obviously done to showboat his physical impairments. I was not aware, until this moment, that a 'messed-up shoulder' manifested itself in one's legs!

As he passes us, Kerry shouts, 'YOU LIAR!' but she is not taken to task for it. There is no reaction whatsoever from Little. He is unfazed because he is well protected. I am sure he is rather proud of his performance.

It's the end of a horrendous day, one which saw Ray and others storm out of the court at times. Hearing Little say that Rachel had consensual sex with him was too much for Mark, her heartbroken sweetheart. Similarly affected were her father and brother on hearing the graphic account of how she was stabbed to death. I managed to endure it all, but each of us is in a terrible state at this point – physically and emotionally drained, nervous wrecks. But nothing compares to what our beloved girl went through before she died.

A few words with our barrister before we leave for the day. Lots of encouragement from him, the leading detectives and the CPS. They all seem confident. Tomorrow, we are assured, will come the closing speeches and, following that, the judge's summing up. All seems to be going to plan and the junior prosecutor believes that two or three more days should see an end to it. We can hope for a verdict before the end of this week. Thank the Lord.

Wednesday, 22 October 2003
– Day Seven

O ur routine is set by now. We, the immediate family, arrive at the court together and meet up with Ronnie, Mark and his mother once there. Friends and once or twice my brother Paul and his wife have joined us. The media are still keeping their vigil, both inside the courtroom and outside on the concourse. We are well used to them by now.

There is an eerie atmosphere when we arrive today and, for no particular reason, I feel most uneasy. We are summoned into court one and see the prosecution and defence teams in deep conversation. The jury have not yet been called and we have already seen some of the police leaving in a hurry.

Kerry thinks she has heard the phrase 'a fly in the ointment' being bandied about. We are puzzled and a little afraid when she tells us this. Mr Marson addresses Judge Hooper to request that the jury not be brought in for the moment, since a problem has arisen. Whatever this problem is, it requires a discussion between the defence, prosecution and judge and will be heard in chambers. Court is dismissed and we all go outside in a most unsettled state.

Before too long, we are told that nothing will be happening today so everyone will be sent home. The trial is being held up for legal reasons. What a shock and what can these reasons be?

Seriously worried, we all file out and at length our barrister has a brief word with us. He seems much less buoyant than usual and can give us little information about the hold-up, aside from the fact that there isn't just one fly in the ointment – there are three! He looks concerned but does his best to reassure us, saying that the first of the problems has already been addressed and the second is in the process of being so. As regards the third, we can only wait and see. It sounds ominous.

Ray is in a very bad way, so he is taken aside by the leading detective and given a brief resume of what is actually going on. After this, Ray seems a little easier in his mind but, since he has been sworn to secrecy, he is unable to take us into his confidence. All he will say is that, on balance, nothing has really altered. The facts remain as ever they did and he feels better for having spoken with the detective. Well, at least one of us does, then! Ray has a lot of integrity and, having been asked to keep the information divulged to himself, he will do so. We, in turn, would not attempt to ask him to break this promise – it would not be fair.

It has been a wasted and frustrating day. We had been expecting to see light at the end of the tunnel but instead we are faced with uncertainty and fear. Still, we can do nothing about it, so we return home.

Thursday, 23 October 2003
– Day Eight

A stressful night has finally passed and we are all nervous when we reach court, with the exception of Ray, who already knows what lies in store. While waiting on the concourse to enter the courtroom, I am told by a volunteer that a young man has arrived to give evidence. I am puzzled that another witness has been called at this stage but she assures me not to worry; he is here for the prosecution. We soon discover that she is wrong and that he will speak on behalf of the defence – Little's first and only witness. It doesn't sound too good to me. This was the reason, then, for yesterday's delay. Small wonder our team had all looked so concerned.

Into court, then, in time to see Mr Kadri girding his loins. He is almost dancing with delight at this turn of events and even Little, when he shows his face, looks hopeful. I am beside myself with fear now. Surely nothing can happen at this stage to change things? Not after we have endured so much …

The first witness this day is the officer to whom Jim, the young man, had casually divulged this latest evidence. He has a very smart, almost military bearing, instilling confidence immediately in those watching. According to his notes, Jim spoke of someone entering the house next door at around midnight. Marc Fuller lived in the house next door. Jim heard the door open and close, but saw nobody. While looking out of his bedroom window, Jim said he then saw someone leave the house at, according to the officer's notes, 1.45am. If this were so, it could not have been Marc on the CCTV footage at 1am that morning – not if he were still at home three-quarters of an hour later and had been there since midnight!

At once, Mr Kadri goes to work on the PC, trying hard to refute his notes. He claims that a mistake has been made and, in fact, Jim had said the person left the house at 12.45am and not 1.45am, as written down. This officer, however, is not one to be rattled by Mr Kadri. He insists that he recorded everything correctly and did so as soon as his conversation with Jim was over, so there was no time to forget what was said. In any event, Marc still could not have covered almost six miles between 12.45am and 1am!

There is a hush as Jim appears to take the stand. A stocky young man of 21 years, he has a baby face and a very nervous manner. Mr Kadri has first crack of the whip and makes the most of it, painting Jim in a saintly light. One could be forgiven for thinking he is no more than an upright citizen doing his duty. The strange thing is that, given all the publicity Rachel's case has generated for many months, Jim's memory was only jogged a day ago.

Aided and abetted by Mr Kadri, Jim puts himself across as a mild-mannered, teetotal family man who, together with his partner and child, just happened to be next door over the holidays. He tells the court of his achievements, of working in the community and helping youngsters. It all sounds very commendable and above board. Nothing untoward here, it would seem.

We are now greatly shocked by Mr Marson's opening words. Standing, he begins to read out a list of convictions. It seems Jim's cherubic appearance masks what lies beneath. The misdemeanours range from criminal damage to assault. Some go way back, but his latest court appearance is a mere few months ago. Probably the most unbelievable is his beating up and later shooting a teacher! We hear that a 13-year-old child was hit at the same time. This young man is, in fact, no stranger to the courts.

When pressed about his last court appearance, in February 2003, he maintains that he can recall little about it; he cannot remember if he pleaded guilty or not. He does, however, remember the make and number of the rifle with which he shot his teacher, several years previously. He was eventually expelled from school following numerous suspensions and never completed his education.

We all gasp at what follows: 'Isn't it a fact that there is a long-standing feud between your family and Marc's?'

Seemingly, this concerns a dispute over a garden fence and we are further shocked to learn that in April 2003, only six months ago, there had been an altercation involving Marc and the partner of Jim's mother. Marc had retaliated by punching this man on the nose. Marc was given a caution over this, though Jim says that he knew nothing about it. It is up to the jury to consider what they make of all this.

We can only hope this will be the end of it and the closing

speeches can finally take place. I cannot imagine that anyone would want it to drag on indefinitely but the defence are not going to give in that easily. Having Jim turn up at the eleventh hour has given them an unexpected bonus and the opportunity to perhaps put a doubt in the minds of the jurors. Mr Kadri stands to address the court and, in no uncertain terms, demands that the case be closed and a retrial be held. Why should his client sit accused of murder, when the real murderer walks free? He demands that the police reopen the case, investigate Marc more thoroughly and charge *him* with the crime.

This is most upsetting, not to mention frightening. What if that really were to happen? God forbid that we should have to go through all of this again!

For once, fate smiles on us. The judge is not going to let this happen and Mr Kadri will just have to be satisfied with his decision but he does not seem happy and will not give in. To give credit where it is due, he has gone over and above the call of duty in his efforts to get Little acquitted.

He recalls Marc, his mother and sister, in order to question them all once more in light of Jim's evidence. He would also like the witness brought back from Spain, though this is not deemed feasible. It is obviously his prerogative to recall these people but it seems to me that he is only prolonging the agony. Little can be gained by all this and it will have to end at some point. It all seems cruel and unnecessary.

In the afternoon, we are told that Marc's mother has arrived at court and his sister is on her way. Marc himself has not yet been located but the police are out searching for him at this moment. That shouldn't pose too big a problem for the defence. Our barrister asks if, in Marc's absence, his mother and sister can be questioned now, as they have no idea as to why they have been brought back and both are in a bad way.

Mr Kadri is having none of this. He insists that he question them in the same order as before and that means that Marc must be first. So for us it is another wasted half-day. We must return home and wait to see what tomorrow brings. Our nerves are stretched tight and starting to fray. Everything seems to be spiralling out of control.

Friday, 24 October 2003
– Day Nine

Another day dawns and the second week is all but over. I am sure that none of us expected things to go on for this long, nor would they have done but for Jim's last-minute appearance. I should say at this point that the first two flies in the ointment were really nothing at all – just rumours and gossip that were quickly sorted out by the police and proved to be groundless. In fact, the police were under no legal obligation to call Jim to give evidence when they did. Technically, the closing speeches could have gone ahead because both prosecution and defence had closed their cases. It was felt, however, that his evidence should be heard, in all fairness to the defence. If nothing else, there could be no reason afterwards for an appeal, once all aspects had been addressed and discounted. I must agree.

The first person to appear this morning is Marc who, not knowing why he has been recalled, is no less angry than he was on his debut.

When asked by Mr Marson if he knows what is behind this latest turn of events, he answers no. Despite his annoyance and vitriol, it is easy to see he is frightened. Mr Marson does not attempt to enlighten him, merely asking him the same questions as before: his movements on the night of 31 December, the time at which he left the party he was at, when he arrived home, etc. It is just a repeat of his first appearance in court and his answers are the same as they were then.

Even though Mr Marson is kindly towards him, Marc is still swearing and abusive. The judge is forced to ask him to behave on more than one occasion but is nonetheless more than lenient with him. I am sure that he is becoming more perplexed by the minute, still not grasping what he is actually doing back here.

Mr Kadri is about to enlighten him and I want to remain in court this time. He struts forward and takes sweeping glances around the room before he begins. I can tell he is going to enjoy his moment, as he goes immediately for the throat.

Marc's previous testimony is dissected in minute detail, as Mr Kadri tries to trip him up at every turn. He challenges the time he arrived home, whether his sister was or wasn't there already, even the clothes he was wearing. Some very heated exchanges take place and I listen in horrified fascination.

Marc's language is choice. For every challenge or insult that is thrown his way, he comes back with one of his own. It's electrifying! On one occasion, Mr Marson has to stand up and protest to the judge. It is inconceivable that a witness can be treated in such a way, when no charge stands against him. At one point, Mr Kadri shouts at Marc, 'Are you going to stab *me*?' I wouldn't have his job for all the tea in China.

Marc seems genuinely amazed when told that someone,

identified as him, had been seen leaving his house early on New Year's morning, and that the witness was a young man living next door to him. He was not aware there *was* a young man in residence next door and asks his age. Jim had already admitted that Marc was not known to him, he just knew *of* him.

In spite of Mr Kadri's valiant efforts to make him say otherwise, Marc does not deviate from his original testimony. Mr Kadri is frustrated and thwarted at every turn. There are, however, a few light moments when Marc, though rude and abusive, really puts him in his place. I think everyone enjoys that and feels like giving the lad a round of applause, especially when he tells Mr Kadri he is 'a stupid little man'!

When he is finally allowed to stand down and is thanked by the judge, Marc turns and fires one final round of expletives, this time at Little. He calls him a 'f***ing murdering bastard'. Little does not flinch at this tirade.

Marc's mother and sister are again brought back into court, one after the other. They are both as in the dark as Marc was about why they have been recalled. The police have told them nothing so what must they be thinking at this latest twist?

Mr Marson does no more than repeat his questions from last time. What more can he do? He does not have to cast a shadow of doubt on what they have already said. Mr Kadri, however, does and goes about it in his own inimitable way. They get the full treatment at length and again both retire in tears.

I need to keep reminding myself that it is the defence's job to interrogate witnesses in this manner but it is very hard to warm towards this man. At least all three stood their ground under intense pressure and we can be thankful that not one of them changed their story from the original.

We are due a short recess now, a much-needed one after this morning's shenanigans. Later today, we may see some more, for we are now aware of what is in store and await it with eager trepidation.

Because the defence played this card, the prosecution are to retaliate. Jim is being brought back for further questioning, which seems fair enough to me. This is expected to happen this afternoon and meanwhile the court adjourns for lunch. We have a lot to talk about for the next hour and we need to analyse what has transpired so far today. On the whole, none of us is too disturbed by the events of the morning and we are beginning to feel quite hopeful once more. We wonder how Jim will be feeling at the prospect of a second appearance. Not happy, with a bit of luck.

We don't have long to wonder, as he is brought into court as soon as lunch is over. Like the three before him this morning, he has no idea why he is back. Our barrister makes short work of him and in no time at all Jim is confused and contradicting himself at every turn. He is clearly very worried. I hope that we can finally get on with the next stage of the proceedings.

When Jim leaves the stand, the judge decides to call it a day. It's mid-afternoon on Friday and he feels the jury has heard enough. We can all go home for the weekend and prepare ourselves for next week, the third of this trial. On Monday will come the closing speeches from both sides, followed by the judge's summing up. We shall need all our resources to cope with the next few days.

It proves to be an uneventful weekend, though not without a few concerns from other quarters. Kerry has already had to drive home and back again once while the trial progressed.

Now things are even more difficult for her. Having left three children for two weeks so far, she is reluctant to do so for even longer. It is unthinkable, though, that, having sat through all of this, she should miss the final outcome. It is, after all, what she has been here for, and her presence has been indescribably appreciated.

Ronnie, too, has cancelled his flight back to Ireland twice now. Whatever happens, he must return on Wednesday night. He has commitments of his own at home. I cannot imagine how we are all going to feel if either of them is absent when the verdict is announced.

Monday, 27 October 2003
– Day Ten

Another show of solidarity on this, the first day of the third week. We, Rachel's family and friends, are very much in tune with each other's feelings now. This thing has brought us all close in a way I could never have imagined. It is so good to reach out a hand and to know that there is always someone there to take it, to understand what you are experiencing. This feeling of unity, I believe, can only be understood by those who have been in such a situation themselves.

We expect this day to be taken up with the closing speeches, with little real hope of the judge getting round to his summing up. As the prosecuting barrister, Mr Marson will begin. He speaks very well, very eloquently and puts his case across firmly. I think he covers every aspect and I notice, not for the first time, how suave he is, how urbane and in control of himself. I only hope that he has put our case across in a strong enough manner to convince the jury of Little's guilt.

Time seems to pass quickly as we all listen intently to his words so it's rather a surprise to look at the clock and see just how long his speech has lasted. There is no way that the defence lawyer will have time for his speech this morning. It looks like we will all be sent out for lunch a bit earlier than usual but we need the time out to psych ourselves up for Mr Kadri and whatever he has to throw at us.

The stroll across to the pub over the road has become second nature to us by now. It's just some place to spend the recess, as opposed to remaining in the courthouse, or venturing into the city centre, neither of which really appeals.

Mr Kadri is raring to go, no sooner than the proceedings under way. We've observed his performance for over two weeks now and are quite sure he is about to pull out all the stops on this, his final onslaught. It's his last chance to get Little off the hook and I don't relish what we are about to witness.

When seen outside of the courtroom, Mr Kadri looks very insignificant. Wigless and minus his gown, he passes as your everyday man in the street. However, once attired for action, he takes on a new and quite frightening persona, almost like a bird of prey about to swoop. In my heightened state of tension, it feels like he is homing in on me alone, as he immediately goes to work.

In the early part of his speech, he concentrates on Marc, trying his utmost to make the jury believe that he is the one who really ought to be on trial. One could be fooled into thinking that he is actually the co-accused, instead of a person against whom no charge has ever been levelled. His voice rises dramatically as, pointing his finger at Little, he declares that his client is the innocent party. He again pushes the issue of a retrial, with Marc in the dock in place of Little. He once more infers that the police did not take their investigation far enough and should be made to do so now.

I find his words frightening, even though I know for certain that the right man is already in the dock.

Mr Kadri presses on relentlessly and really starts to hit hard. I am finding it hard to sit here as he begins his next line of defence, which, to my despair, turns out to be nothing more or less than a character assassination of Rachel.

With the appearance of everyone's favourite uncle, he smiles benignly at the jury and says, 'Now, I know my client is a fat slob – he won't mind me saying so because that is how he describes himself. But he is not so repulsive that he couldn't get a girl.'

What is this leading up to? I soon find out.

'We have heard that Rachel was in a steady relationship.' Mr Kadri pauses and takes a sweeping look around the courtroom, in particular at the public gallery. 'It is not unheard of for someone to go astray. Indeed, even married women have been known to do so.'

What a scurrilous comment and coming from one who knows nothing of Rachel, a further insult. How dare he sully her memory in this way and do it with a smile and a shrug of the shoulders?

More salt is rubbed into the wound as he continues, making little of the phone calls I made that morning, by saying, 'And, as for the phone calls, well, she could have chosen to ignore them, had her own reasons for not wishing to answer.'

No mention, though, that his client denied their very existence. Rachel is dead, she was murdered and yet this man is compounding our grief by implying that she wasn't up to much anyway.

Ray is in such a fury that he can hardly be held down. His voice is clearly audible as he states, in no uncertain terms, what he will do to this man. So angry and upset is he that he storms out of the courtroom, followed by several others, though I stay put.

I am hardly aware of the remainder of Mr Kadri's rhetoric as I sit with my head in my hands, unable to look at his face as he continues to blacken my daughter. She is not on trial here. All this is being done to justify Michael Little's actions on that night. Were it even remotely true that Rachel had chosen to consort with a 'slob', it did not give him licence to murder her.

I am almost alone now in the public gallery and I must seem distraught because one of the Victim Support volunteers comes up behind me. She obviously thinks I am crying because I am covering my face but she is wrong. I am filled with total and utter rage.

Outside on the concourse, I find Ray in a terrible state and surrounded by lots of people. He has to be physically restrained, as he wants only to get hold of Mr Kadri. Our two girls are trying hard to calm him down. John is wise enough to stay clear. Ray is trying to grab Ronnie's walking stick.

What a terrible scenario before me and I am loath to interfere. I know my husband and his temper but I try to reason with him anyway, without success. He is almost out of control and, in desperation, Kerry runs back into the courtroom to ask that Mr Kadri is not allowed to come out by way of the concourse.

After a while, we see him being escorted out by the police and taken into a back room. He is kept there until we all leave the building and it's just as well; I can't be responsible for

Ray's actions this day. I am terrified, even as we go to pick up the car, in case we encounter Mr Kadri and his team on the street. More than anything, I don't want to jeopardise the case at this late stage. I can, however, fully understand Ray's reaction to what was said. Any father would feel the same under similar circumstances. I, as Rachel's mother, feel no less furious. We have to keep telling ourselves that this is not personal, it is simply the job of the defence. He has to do and say whatever it takes to win his case.

It will be almost impossible for any of us to settle tonight after what we have had to sit through in court today. Perhaps we can be forgiven if we need a couple of drinks before we retire?

Tuesday, 28 October 2003
– Day Eleven

Media interest is whipping up now as this could be the last day of the trial. More cameras than usual await us on the courthouse steps, hoping for a scoop I would guess.

As has been the norm, court resumes at 10am, but today, to our amazement, only ticket-holders can enter the courtroom! This in itself makes one realise the enormity of the situation. I am trying hard not to think of these coming hours, of the interminable wait for the jury to return a verdict. Meanwhile, though, there is still the judge's summing up to come, and, after that, it will be in the lap of the gods.

Judge Hooper is obviously very learned, one of the top men in the country and, I would say, a compassionate one. Above all, he sticks to the letter of the law. Not once does he try to lead the jury; he merely goes through the evidence, explaining everything in depth. It is very easy to follow his words. There are no complicated issues and the jury appear to take in all he is saying. I believe they are taking their role very seriously. Even so, there are times when I feel he appears overly fair in favour of the defence's case. Is this my imagination, I wonder. Perhaps I expected that, due to the evidence against Little, he would have gravitated more towards the prosecution when summing up.

His speech seems to go on forever, continuing after the lunch recess but, because his words are so crucial, time flies and I see no signs of boredom from his audience. Probably the only one who seems detached from it all is Michael Little. He sits with eyes closed throughout.

Towards the middle of the afternoon, the jury are sent out to deliberate and everyone else leaves the courtroom. We adjourn to the concourse, some to smoke, others for refreshments, but all to worry. Nobody believes that the jury will be out for too long. In fact, I am sure that we are expecting a verdict this very afternoon.

I have already decided that I will not enter the courtroom to hear the verdict so I shall remain on the concourse, whatever happens from now on. Some have questioned my decision in this matter, even said that Rachel would have wanted me there, but I am not swayed. I simply cannot go in there, cannot risk a not guilty verdict, however unlikely that may seem. I could not look into the face of Rachel's murderer should he be set free. This is my final decision and I am standing by it. Each time there is an announcement on the tannoy, my heart turns over, but I sit firm. Lorraine, Mark's mother, feels as I do, so I will not be alone. She will be with me the entire time.

Two hours have passed without a word. I suppose it was too much to expect that the jury would return so soon but I feel somewhat disappointed and fearful because they have not. At almost 4pm, the judge calls everyone back into court for the final time today. The jury are sent home. Obviously, they are nowhere near their verdict and, in all truth, a couple of hours is no length of time in which to arrive at such a monumental decision. Perhaps we were all too optimistic to expect more. Tomorrow is another day.

Wednesday, 29 October 2003
– Day Twelve

Even more media attention this morning and an air of expectation prevails. To say we are nervous is a vast understatement. Today we are terrified. It will be hard, whatever happens, since Ronnie is to travel back to Ireland this evening. Kerry is expected home today also. Her husband has coped with the three children for two and a half weeks now, as well as going into work each day. How cruel it will be, though, if these two, who have been such towers of strength to us, are unable to be with us when the verdict is announced.

Although I have my entry ticket, I have no use for it, since I will not be going into court. As usual, our friends are gathered here for us and we sit in small groups around the concourse. Each time the loudspeaker sounds, my heart skips a beat, each time wondering if this is it and each time it is not.

The tension is unbearable and, as the hours pass, it becomes more so. Periodically, the judge calls the jury back in and asks if they have reached a decision and, on every occasion, I experience a further rush of adrenaline. The morning drags on, and on and on. At this point, none of us seems capable of comforting one another, as we are all so overwrought with tension and fear.

During this time, I have a brief conversation with one of our liaison officers. She looks quite concerned and asks if anyone has explained to me what a hung jury means. No, and, until this minute, such a thing had never entered my head! Her explanation throws me into a panic and I do wonder if she is preparing me for the worst.

I do know what a unanimous verdict is, when all 12 jurors agree, and have recently learned that a majority decision must be no less than 10–2 or 11–1. What is a surprise to me is that a split greater than that is classed as a hung jury. In my ignorance, I thought that it had to be six for and six against. Now I know how the odds are stacked, I start to fear the worst. This is not a good time for me to be given this information and this little talk has done nothing to boost my confidence. Even among this crowd of people, I feel so alone and so afraid. There is nothing that anyone could say or do that would help me at this present moment.

Another announcement on the PA and another false alarm. Something, surely, has gone wrong. The atmosphere is unbearable and not only we but also the police, CPS and the media are all in a state of high tension. The outcome means so much to so many.

Ray is pacing the floor: he is in a pitiable state and wants nobody near him. Father White is here but he, too, can do nothing to comfort any of us and sits with his eyes closed, seemingly in prayer. Well, that's fine by me — we need every prayer we can get!

Lunchtime arrives and still no verdict. I overhear a conversation between two of the police team and am immediately thrown into a panic. It seems obvious from their words that the jury are still undecided and that the judge has told them he will now accept a majority verdict. Even the police appear nervous now, which does not augur well for the rest of us. The jury have been out for about six hours, in a case where it was expected the verdict would be reached in no more than one or two. But the ball is in the jury's court and we can do nothing at all about it except worry and fret. This really is nail-biting time.

The lunch break is horrendous. My sister-in-law has run from her work in the city centre, fully expecting to hear some positive news and is disappointed. She cannot believe that there is still no decision, nor can we. I take some comfort from her words of encouragement, however, and am sorry that she can't stay with us for the rest of today's ordeal.

Ray wishes to be alone and walks down to the sea front. I don't want him to do this: I feel I should be with him but it is his choice and I must respect it. Rather unwillingly, I adjourn to the nearest hostelry with the rest of the family and friends. I am very worried about my husband in his present state of distress and for one hysterical moment I think he might throw himself into the River Humber. I am too afraid to eat anything and it all seems so unreal. My fears are unfounded though, as, when we leave the pub, I see him heading back towards the courthouse. We meet up and enter the court together, drawing strength from each other for this, the final push. Or so we hope ...

This afternoon is no less fraught than this morning and possibly more so, as the minutes tick by. For me, this is the worst day of my life, strange as that may sound. Worse than the time Rachel went missing, for then I had no time to sit around weeping. Worse even than the fateful day when her body was found. I was much too stunned then to let go. This feeling of extreme terror is worse by far than anything I have ever experienced in my life and I would not wish it on my very worst enemy — unless, of course, it was Michael Little.

My state of mind is such that I could run out of this building, never to return. But that would be a coward's way out so I must hold myself together for Rachel's sake. What would she think of a mother who couldn't take the pressure, when she had had to suffer so very much more?

The interminable call of the public address system is beginning to sound like a death knell by now. I welcome yet dread it, each time wondering if this is the verdict and, when it is not, experiencing a feeling of relief. Not only am I shaking like a leaf but I am physically sick and feel sure that this is how most of the others are feeling, For our agony to be prolonged in this manner is the cruellest irony of all.

Just as I think that I can truly stand no more of this, an announcement is made. It is mid-afternoon on day ten, well into the second day of deliberation. Surely this *must* be the verdict? Everyone rushes into court one, apart from Lorraine and I, but they are quite quickly out again.

Ray walks towards me and he doesn't seem too upset, which can only be a good sign. He says that the jury have asked to see the CCTV footage again and also want to take a closer look at Rachel's clothing. I start to fret at once, not knowing which footage he is referring to but, when told it is the tape from the school, I relax slightly. My mind is working overtime at this turn of events. It must surely mean that they are close to a decision and I dare to let myself think that it must be in our favour. I can see no reason for them wanting one last look at these two exhibits except to dispel all doubt from their minds. To confirm that it was indeed Michael Little on the film and to see the severity of Rachel's wounds, by way of her dress and jacket. What else could it mean?

Some time elapses while the jury are viewing Rachel's clothes at close quarters in a private room. I don't envy them. Meanwhile, a television is being set up to facilitate the viewing of the CCTV. Anyone is free to enter the courtroom while it is being shown, but I choose to remain out on the concourse to try to digest what this latest occurrence might mean. I also try to calm myself down in preparation for what is yet to come, because it is not over by a long way.

At length, the courtroom empties yet again and we continue our waiting game. My heart is racing as the loudspeaker jumps to life, almost like an imam calling the faithful to prayer. I imagine that *this* can only be the verdict now as everyone files back into court one. In no time at all, though, they are back out on the concourse and the body language says it all; there will be no verdict this day. The judge has sent the jury home for the night. He feels that they have had more than enough for one day. If they have experienced even a jot of the tension that we have over the past few hours, I am inclined to agree with him. They will return in the morning at 10am.

Although I know it is only delaying the inevitable, I feel

almost light-hearted that no decision has been reached. It means that, while there is no good news, there is no bad either. Silly really, but I feel like I have escaped the hangman's noose, at least for the time being.

Now comes the hard part. Ronnie has to fly home tonight and he is distraught as we prepare to leave the courthouse. He is terribly, terribly upset that he has to leave us and will definitely not be here for the final verdict. He has made friends during his stay, and got to know the police team, CPS and some of the journalists. He has been a massive support to us all, especially to Ray, and we are devastated at his departing.

Kerry, too, ought to return to Southampton, but, after a quick phone call, her husband has no objections to her staying here for one more day. Tomorrow, surely, must be *the* day?

Nobody is really in a fit state to drive Ronnie to Leeds airport, but Kerry volunteers anyway. She really has been great through all of this. However, our good old friend Father White will not hear of it and offers to do the journey himself. Ray will accompany him and this seems the best solution by far. So, we say our tearful farewells to Ronnie and promise to let him know the very second we have some news.

After this terrible, traumatic and most horrendous of days, I am completely shattered. I can do no more than sink into the bathtub, after which I fall exhausted into my bed at 9.30pm. I am asleep even before Ray gets home.

Thursday, 30 October 2003 – Day Thirteen

Following the terror of yesterday, I feel a little better today, more positive and hopeful. I am at peace with myself for the moment, but I don't expect that to last. I take comfort when my son comes downstairs and offers a few words of encouragement. I want desperately to believe him when he tells me that everything will be OK. I need to convince myself that it will be so and, on seeing a robin outside in the garden, it does seem like an omen. I tell myself that Rachel has sent him as a sign that she will be with us today and that all will be well.

This morning I go with Ray to the cemetery. At Rachel's graveside, we tell her that this is the day, the one we have waited for and the one in which we hope that justice will be done for her. I feel very close to her at this moment and her spirit is all-enveloping. Stay with me through this day, Rach, and give me the strength I will need to keep going, should the very worst happen.

Then it's back home and time to face the day. We can do no more than place our trust in God and hope that common sense will prevail.

The media once more await us on our arrival at the courthouse and seem even more psyched up than they were yesterday. Several large TV vans are here, in addition to the usual cameramen and journalists, ready to tell the world at large the story as it breaks. Let us hope that it does so in the next few hours.

Court is due to sit at 10am and again I refuse to enter the courtroom itself. Not only Lorraine but Kerry, too, decides that she will stay outside with me for support. I feel very guilty on hearing this, since I know that she did want to hear the verdict first hand. I am grateful for her loyalty to me.

When the call for Michael Little's case is announced, there is a frantic dash towards court one. Extra seats have been set out for the many journalists but some members of the public try to gain entry and are turned away. Tickets are limited and these folk, who I have not seen before, don't have any. I do wonder if any of them are relatives of Michael Little but decide probably not. Not one has appeared so far and these few people, it turns out, are just the curious. Having read about the case, they want a glimpse of this vile creature for themselves. I'm not sure that I would want to if I were not so closely involved, but it takes all kinds, or so they say.

Very soon, everyone comes out again and I understand that Michael Little has not arrived in court yet. There has been an accident en route from Doncaster and the van transporting him has been held up. In my wild state of emotion, it crosses my mind that he might have tried to do away with himself now that the chips are down. No such luck. It's traffic problems, pure and simple.

The judge has asked both counsels if they will agree to the jury deliberating in Little's absence and neither has any objection to this. We don't know when he is likely to arrive and I am in a very bad state by now. I am rigid with fear, the buoyancy I felt earlier totally diminished, and it is no help to hear that the judge has given the jury until 11am to come up with a result. If they are not unanimous by then, he will accept a majority verdict. Things are looking very black to me.

Despite the hive of activity going on all around, an ethereal feeling abounds and a strange, eerie silence prevails among us. Numerous people are glancing in our direction, all knowing what we are waiting for. The press are on red alert, cameras poised at the ready, mobile phones and laptops to the fore.

I am huddled on a bench, Lorraine at one side and Kerry at the other. I feel myself starting to shake uncontrollably. My arms and legs tingle and I feel on the point of collapse. It is a very physical reaction and I am very frightened. I always considered myself a sensible person, in control of myself, but now I am rapidly losing it, to my shame and horror.

Suddenly, without any announcement, everyone starts to rush towards court one. Press, police and ushers – they all dash along and the family follows at speed. Only Kerry, Lorraine and myself are left behind. Something must have caused this mass exodus and obviously Little must have arrived too by now. This is the most heart-stopping moment ever. Nothing can prevent what must surely ensue: this has to be the verdict!

It is exactly 10.50am. It seems no more than a few minutes pass before the doors burst open. Running towards us is one of the volunteers, who has kept us fortified with drinks for the duration. She is in tears, but this tells me nothing – it could mean anything, good or bad. Kerry, however, has spotted a CPS assistant approaching with a smile on her face and we hear the word 'guilty' being shouted all around us!

The three of us, by now in hysterical tears of relief, hasten into the courtroom at once. So out of control am I that I fall into the first empty seat that I see and am comforted, not by any family member or friend, but by a complete stranger. He is a member of the public, unknown to us, but who has been here every day throughout the trial. I am vaguely aware of him holding me tightly, until my senses return and I am able to stop shaking. Some very strange and worried looks come from the police team; they have never seen me give way like this before. Perhaps they think that I have finally cracked under pressure. Perhaps I have.

Eventually, I compose myself enough to realise that our counsel, Mr Marson, is now reading out the statement that I had written beforehand. I have already missed the reading of Mark's personal statement. Mr Marson seems very moved as he reads out my words, as are the police, the CPS, ushers and volunteers alike. All of these people have been with us throughout the trial, many of them since the beginning of our ordeal way back in January.

I sense people weeping all around me, though Ray is not. He sits with his eyes tightly closed but looks totally distraught. Mark is heartbroken. He had threatened to run amok should Little walk free and there is a large police presence in case of such an occurrence. Indeed, the judge has already warned against any outbursts but I feel we are all behaving very well, under the circumstances.

I look directly at Little as the judge finally speaks. He first asks Little to stand up but he does not do so. Maybe he doesn't hear or understand but he has to be asked three times before he is finally brought to his feet. Not one trace of emotion crosses his face as the judge sentences him to life imprisonment, adding that in his case life may well mean just that. Small comfort to us. Nothing is ever going to bring Rachel back, nor compensate for the terror he put her through. My poor, poor girl, my sweet baby child.

The defence barrister is asked to comment on behalf of his client and can say only that this was, indeed, a most wicked and evil crime but adds that, since this is a young man, it would help if he could see light at the end of the tunnel. The only light I want Michael Little to see is the fire of Hell. The judge makes no comment on Mr Kadri's suggestion.

There is a lot of satisfaction when Little is given a life sentence and stands waiting to be taken away. He really does appear to be momentarily stunned and that is very gratifying for me. The tables are turned now and, hopefully, he will soon know how it feels to be the prey, as opposed to the hunter. Did he seriously think that he would go free? In my heart of hearts, and despite my fears, I always knew he would not. God could not be so cruel a second time.

There's an even happier moment when the judge rules that he is quite certain that Rachel did not have consensual sex with this monster. At last, my girl is exonerated in court and my cup runneth over. Rachel *was* an innocent party in all this and, by whatever means, Little took her by force — a fact that we, and the police, had always felt sure was true. It is so good to hear the judge agreeing with us and it means as much to me as the guilty verdict, if not more.

One last look at Little as he is led away. Still no emotion and no attempt is made to glance in our direction. He truly is a fiend and to think that his face was the last one my daughter saw ... He lived like a normal person and appeared as one but beneath he was really a devil incarnate, and none of us recognises the devil on our doorstep.

The police boss, Detective Superintendent Paul Davison, who has been in charge since day one, is asked to take the stand now, to explain to the court how he set about the whole operation. I don't know if this is normal procedure, as he seems rather surprised when asked to do this. How gut-wrenching to see this strong, fearless man, who took so many risks on Rachel's behalf, reduced to tears. Not only he, but also his entire team are visibly moved by now. Maybe it's relief but it is genuine. There is hardly a dry eye in the room as he tries to speak. The judge asks him to explain a little about the investigation, the decisions he made and the reasons for those decisions.

Mr Davison is quick to give credit to his team and names some of them in particular. So emotional is he now that he can hardly speak as, with shaking hands, he sips from a cup of water. I know now that which I have felt from the start: that Rachel was not just a statistic to these people. She was real, they felt that they knew her through their involvement with us and they craved justice both for her and for us, her family and loved ones. I give thanks to each and every one of the team concerned, to the CPS and to our barrister, Mr Marson. Without him, today's conclusion might never have been reached. It has finally come to pass: a very poignant moment and one I shall remember always.

At this point, the judge makes several recommendations. He will be writing to the Chief Constable in order that they be implemented. It is good to know that all of the hard work put into the case will not go unrecognised.

And so we leave court one for the last time. In some ways, this room has become a part of us, but this is a chapter of our lives that we would never wish to relive.

We step out on to the crowded concourse to be greeted by a sea of faces. Those of us who have mobile phones are trying to send text messages or make calls to friends and relatives at home and elsewhere. Everyone will be waiting with bated breath to hear from us, even though by now the news will have gone out far and wide. Most of the journalists ran from court the minute the verdict was read out. A few euphoric moments up here, people to meet and thank, and we badly need to compose ourselves before we face the media. Then it's downstairs and out on to the courthouse steps, where we are bombarded by cameras and reporters, all of whom want to speak to us.

'There is no elation, no victory, no forgiveness, only emptiness.' These are the words read out by Kerry, on the steps of the courthouse. Words we had composed earlier but words we dared not assume would be spoken. There was no alternative statement ready, had the verdict not gone in our favour.

Cameras flash and microphones are thrust in front of us. The city revolves all around but we are oblivious to it. Our moment, Rachel's moment, has finally arrived, exactly ten months after Michael Little was charged with her murder. We savour the moment: the sorrowing will come later. We have a lifetime in which to grieve and we will do so, each one of us in our own way.

On this cool October morning, we take some time to speak with and be filmed and then photographed by the media. We owe them this much for their constancy, and in particular we are indebted to our own local paper for keeping Rachel's story in the public domain over the last ten months. Now the final chapter must be told and we give it our best shot.

Many passers-by stop to observe the scene; buses and other vehicles slow down and even strangers stop to shake us by the hand. I think the whole of this city and those even further afield will be happy with today's result, but, at the end of the day, all of these good folk can return to their homes and continue their everyday lives. It is we, alone, who will be left to pick up the pieces of our lives – lives that will be forever shattered now that Rachel is no longer here with us. For the moment, though, we are on a high and feel very gratified by the warmth and good wishes we detect all around us.

Eventually, the majority of us cross over the road to the public house that has become our local during the trial. There is no desire to celebrate but we owe it to our supporters and, indeed, it would be churlish in the extreme not to have one last drink together now. A toast to Rachel is given: it is so poignant it brings tears to the eyes. Saoirse, who has been here with us every day, is distraught. She will hold Rachel in her heart always.

There is no joy in this day for Mark, no satisfaction whatsoever, any more than there is for the rest of us. I am heartbroken for him. In his loneliness and despair, he cannot be consoled and Ray is similarly affected.

Time to say our goodbyes now and express our thanks. There is still much to do before the end of this day. The first thing will be to call in at the cemetery to see our girl. We want to tell her that it is all over now. She can sleep tight; her day has come.

There are emotional scenes when we arrive. The word has spread and several people express their good wishes. Others have not heard the verdict until now.

I feel that I have laid my daughter to rest at last and my mind is at ease for the first time since we lost her. I don't, however, expect this feeling to last and have no doubt that, in the morning, everything will fall flat once more.

We cannot loiter, since Kerry is due to drive back home this evening. It is a long and tiring journey at the best of times and she has already had a traumatic day. Before she goes, though, we have one last wish to fulfil, but first, home.

More tears, this time from our neighbours as we arrive at the gates. It seems that the whole of this city is rejoicing at the verdict. Having followed the case from the start and agonising over the last two and a half weeks, everyone is delighted with the result. They are all highly gratified that Michael Little will now be incarcerated, hopefully for the remainder of his life, though we will have to wait some time for the tariff to be set.

So strong is the feeling towards this cowardly individual that there are those in the community who have expressed a wish to kill him personally for what he did to Rachel. Their desire, however, could never be as strong as ours.

One final undertaking remains and, if this is to be

accomplished, a telephone call needs to be made. Ray rings the home of Marc, who has endured so much at the hands of Little in his bid for freedom. We want to visit him before Kerry leaves for home and his mother is happy to agree to our request. It should not take long to drive to them, especially as I am quite familiar with the area.

A lovely, genuine lady welcomes us into her spotless home and greets us warmly. Shortly afterwards, Marc, too, puts in an appearance and we are able to thank him for his bravery in facing the defence so fearlessly. His words and his transparent honesty most definitely helped to damn Little and we shall be eternally grateful to him.

Marc is understandably bitter and has murderous feelings towards Little. His mother less so, even though her life and the lives of the rest of her family have been ruined by this. They too are all victims of one man's wickedness. The ripples caused by his evil are spreading in ever-increasing circles and will continue to do so for many years.

Kerry, though exhausted, must take her leave of us soon and start her long journey home. Ray and I will worry about her until we know she is back safely. We will never be able to thank her enough for her support, both leading up to and during the trial. I, too, owe a similar debt to Vanda, and to John. Rachel would be proud of them all.

Nothing more to do. Ray and I are left here alone, now that Kerry has departed. Vanda is at her own home, accompanied by her good friend Margaret, whose presence we greatly appreciated as a support both to her and us. All this has been too much for Vanda. Physically, she was already in poor shape and the trial has dragged her down even further. Mentally, I know that she is dying inside at the loss of Rachel.

John has remained at the pub with some pals after the verdict was announced. I hope they are drinking to Rachel's memory; I'm sure they will be. He, like the rest of us, has a hard road ahead.

The Aftermath

Time this morning to read some of the newspaper coverage of yesterday's events. In particular, last evening's edition of our own local, the *Hull Daily Mail*. A full front page of Michael Little's face in glorious Technicolor hits me in the eye. The word GUILTY is written above in huge letters. This is the first actual likeness that most people will see of him. Until now, they have had to rely on the court artist's impression. He seems to be staring directly at me and the evil is there for all to see. It is not just I, Rachel's mother, who can recognise this, of that I am sure.

Today, and no doubt again tomorrow, many pages will be given over to him — to what lay behind this monster, his background and how he lived. As I peruse our local paper, I notice comments made by some of those who profess to have known him. They speak of his depravity and their sure knowledge that he was always on course to harm someone.

They crawl out of the woodwork, as is always the case, but none had been asked to give evidence against him, as far as I am aware.

By far the best testimony is that of the lead detective, Paul Davison, given to the press after the trial. Still very emotional by all accounts, he gave his and his team's own views on what they are sure happened to Rachel at the hands of Little. They have always been certain that he 'physically took her off the street', possibly at weapon point, though that cannot be proved. He is even more sure that sex took place post mortem, though, again, that cannot be proved. Because of this, Little was not charged with abduction and rape as well as murder, more's the pity.

However, this is enough to satisfy me and, when these words are seen in print, I hope that the dissenters will now believe that Rachel was, indeed, simply in the wrong place at the wrong time. Although she was in the right place at the right time, walking to her own home. It was Little who was in the wrong place. The knowledge that 99.9 per cent of the population accepted she was an innocent party from the start never took away the fact that there were a few who did not. That tiny minority has been a source of distress to me all along, but is no longer. With these few telling words, Mr Davison has done much to ease my frustration and I am indebted to him.

The one thing that still seriously disturbs and upsets me is that Little's name will be forever linked with Rachel. It seems like some sick, unholy matrimony, as if in a way he got her in the end.

I understand there was anger among the police team at the way in which Marc was brought into play at the hands of the media. I cannot stress strongly enough that the entire police team, men and women, gave this case their all for ten long months. Some did not see their families for days, even weeks on end. They lived and breathed Rachel, and we can never thank them enough for all their hard work in achieving yesterday's result. There is no way they failed to investigate Marc thoroughly, and to suggest otherwise does them all a grave injustice. As Mr Davison says in parting, 'We do not let murderers walk free!'

Coda: Late October to December 2003

After the euphoria at the end of the trial, a period of darkness has descended once more, just as we knew it would. We are all left feeling very deflated now there is nothing to focus on.

More cards, good wishes and flowers still wing their way to our home and there is some relief in being able to discuss, at last, the details with wider family and friends. I am sure many are shocked now they know what happened to Rachel and that we had known much of it all along but had had to keep it to ourselves. There is no denying it was a great strain to do so.

Ray and John are both back at work now, which leaves me alone with lots of time to ponder on things. I still feel unable to return to my own job but, instead, am available to assist Vanda on her numerous hospital appointments each week. At least I am making myself useful and it helps to take my mind off more morbid issues for a time.

The shock of this past year remains: the disbelief and the refusal to accept that such a fate has befallen us all. The unwillingness to face up to the fact that Rachel is gone forever and, even worse, how her demise came about. I am forcing her pain and terror into my subconscious and there it will remain. I think it is the only way I shall ever be able to cope with her passing.

As late November arrives, our own personal 'annus horribilis' is rapidly drawing to a close. Signs of the festive period are everywhere. The days are growing colder, as are our hearts. There is little joy for any of us and we are steeped in misery more often than not.

The only small glimmer of light came earlier this month, when Kerry received her degree in Fine Art from the Southampton Institute. It ought to have been a happy occasion but even that was not to be. Ray, John and I were all due to be at the graduation ceremony, but fate had other plans for us. Halfway into the journey, the car radiator sprang a serious leak and we were forced to return home by courtesy car.

There was no point in trying to complete the trip to Southampton as Ray was feeling very unwell. We would have been poor company, as both John and I were quite worried about Ray's wellbeing. What a big disappointment all round, not least for Kerry, that we would not be there for her big moment. She had put in such a lot of work in the face of great adversity and was left without any family member to support her, apart from her husband and children. The fact that we were so proud of her achievement was, I'm sure, of little consolation to her on that day.

It's December now, and thoughts of Christmas loom on the

horizon, filling me with dread. This is an event into which I always put body and soul to make it happy for everyone. For Rachel, in particular, I always went to great lengths because she loved the occasion so much. At heart, she was still a child. She never really grew up and now she never will. Christmas will be unbearable so we have decided to give it a miss. No tree or decorations for us this year, and perhaps not ever again.

I dare not begin to think about New Year's Eve and how we'll be able to stand it. I cared nothing in the past for the occasion but will detest it even more now. It would be sensible to get right away from here, from this house, this town, even this country. Yet I know that we cannot do so, not on this, Rachel's first anniversary.

Once 2004 is here, there will be another milestone: Rachel's birthday on 17 January. She would be 23. The anger and bitterness are setting in now, as well as the overwhelming sorrow that I cannot cast off. A block of ice occupies the place where once was my heart. I am in deep despair. Dreams of Rachel are with me each night and she is with me in every waking moment, but it brings me no comfort. It is her presence I crave and miss so much. Oh, to be able to turn back the clock, to have handled things differently on that fateful morning, so that she might be here with us still. For us to touch her, kiss her and tell her just how much she is loved. But God does not give second chances …

Epilogue
January 2003

One year has passed since we last saw Rachel. We have survived Christmas, the New Year and her birthday. All of these were very bad times for us but perhaps the worst was New Year's Eve. I counted the hours from dusk till dawn, remembering each event that happened on that terrible day a year before.

Rachel's headstone is now in place at the spot where she lies. It is beautiful, unique and all that I hoped it would be. I know she would approve: 'That's rail [sic] nice, Mam!' Ray still visits her every day and lots of people take the time to stop and say hello to her, often leaving flowers or other little gestures. We are deeply touched by their thoughtfulness.

Her portrait is completed and now takes pride of place in the back lounge. Ryan, the artist, has done a fabulous job, working only from a small photograph. He never met Rachel but he has captured her likeness to a T. Each time I enter the room, I see her smiling down on me, her eyes seeming to follow wherever I go. When I am feeling very low, or have a problem, I speak to her life-sized image and can almost believe she answers me, in her own carefree way.

Even though a painting can never compensate for the reality, it does give me a modicum of comfort – comfort that I especially needed on the sad, bad day when her personal belongings were returned to me. Having to check and then sign for each item recovered was soul-destroying. Seeing the mud on the ones that had been dragged from the drain was particularly stressful for me. Her crucifix now hangs around my own neck and is there to stay, until the day I join Rachel. The other remains of her bright, promising life now lie packed inside two black refuse sacks up in her old room – a terrible, grim reminder of that which was, but was fated never to be.

And so the story of Rachel reaches its end, my story, a mother's story. This is a memory I wanted and needed to share, for myself, for Rachel and for her many family members and friends, some of whom have not yet been born, but all of whom will be able to read this in the passage of time. I ask no more than she is never forgotten.

For many, this will be the final chapter, but not for Ray and myself, her parents. Not for Mark, her first and only love. Certainly not for her sorrowful, grieving sisters and brother, nor for the many people who knew and loved Rachel. There will never, ever be a final chapter for any of us. For the majority of good people in this city of ours, justice has been seen to be done. But, for those of us left behind to grieve for Rachel, justice will never be served, even though the law of the land has been implemented. While the Michael Littles of this world continue to live out their lives in relative comfort, there will be no comfort for us. We are the secondary victims of crimes such as his.

Life as we knew it ended on the eve of New Year 2003 and nothing will ever be the same again. For, in losing Rachel, we have also lost a part of each other and it is hard to imagine there will ever be a light at the end of the tunnel for this family. Little has robbed us, not only of Rachel but also of ourselves. For us there will always be unanswered questions. For us there will never be closure while Rachel's killer continues to protest his innocence. We can never forgive him. *Only God and Rachel can do that.*

I would give my life to know exactly how he lured Rachel into his lair but have accepted that I will probably never find out. At some point in his incarceration, he may decide to say how and why he did what he did. I know, however, that, if that were ever to happen, it would be for his own devious motives, not to help us. In any event, I would not believe anything he might say; a leopard never changes its spots.

Meanwhile, we try not to dwell upon him. Instead, we put our thoughts to better use – to Rachel, to what she stood for, to the joy she brought us and the years we had with her. These can never be taken from us.

Were I to be given the opportunity of confronting the one who took her life, I would only say this to him: 'Wherever you may be incarcerated, I pray that you will never walk free, if only to save the life of another such as Rachel. That you, too, live to dread each waking moment as do we, her family and loved ones. Even as a Christian, I make no excuse for wishing that your life be as unbearable as ours surely will be from now onwards.

'You have stolen from us the most precious of gifts but, in doing so, you have robbed yourself too. Not only will you pay the price by losing the best years of your life, you will never have the joy of knowing the girl who was Rachel. In this, you are the loser, not us.'

I Remember Rachel

So, my beloved child, this part of the tale ends, but, for those of us who are left behind to mourn you, it will never end, while we live.

I have so many happy memories of you, from the moment you drew your first breath. Of you as a baby, a child and, later, a young woman. I cherish them all but memories are not enough because they are not you. You, yourself, are no longer with me, to cheer me up by your presence when I am low. To be part of my future through your own children, to bring comfort to your dad and I as we grow older.

All my hopes and dreams have been shattered because you are no longer here to share them with me. Your own dreams and desires, and those of Mark, will never come to pass now. They all disappeared in one moment of madness. That, above all, is one of the hardest things to bear, and certainly one of the saddest.

I feel your spirit all around me, in every little thing I do. In my waking and in my sleeping, you are always with me, helping me to get through the lonely days and the sleepless nights. I see your face in every rainbow, in the robin who draws near to me in your garden, in every flower that blooms and in the very air that I breathe.

You were with me on that terrible morning when you left this world behind. I heard the choirs of angels singing at what must have been the moment of your departing, and I knew then that I had lost you.

You are with me even as I write these words and you will remain until my final day. Maybe then we shall be together again, in a better place than this cruel world of ours, a world you entered too early and left far too soon.

I am comforted by the fact that you were mine for almost 22 years but it does not take away the pain of your loss. You had so much to offer, so much to give and now there is a void in my life that can never be filled.

Thank you, Rachel, for the privilege of being your mother and for giving me the pleasure of the years I had with you. You will live in my heart forever and, without you, there will be no perfect day. I love you, Rach, and always will.

Sleep tight now and stay close by me, until we meet again. The song is ended but the melody lingers on.

Your broken-hearted Mum xxx

I'll lend you for a little while a child of Mine, God said,
For you to love the while she lives and mourn
for when she's dead.

It may be six or seven years or twenty-two or three,
But will you 'til I call her back take care of her for Me?
She'll bring her charms to gladden you and,
should her stay be brief,

You'll always have her memories as a solace for your grief.
I cannot promise she will stay since all from Earth return,
But there are lessons taught below I want this
child to learn.

I've looked the whole world over in My search
for teachers true,
And from the folks that crowd life's road I
have chosen you.

Now will you give her all your love
nor think the labour vain,
Nor hate Me when I come to take this lent child back again?
I fancied that I heard them say, 'Dear Lord Thy will be done,
For all the joys Thy child will bring
this risk of grief we'll run.

We'll shelter her with tenderness,
we'll love her while we may,
And for the happiness we have known forever grateful stay.

But should the Angels call her
much sooner than we've planned,
We'll brave the bitter grief that comes
and try to understand.'
Anon